Country Girl

by

Nancy Burcham

Library of Congress
Catalog Card Number 76-23907
ISBN: 0-87069-203-8

Published by
Wallace-Homestead Book Co.
Box Bl
Des Moines, Iowa 50304

Table of Contents

Dad's a joker. Anytime, anywhere, we expected anything. Living with Dad led to a lot of laughs, after we learned to laugh at ourselves, down on the farm.

For eleven years the four of us slept in a tiny downstairs bedroom. The two bedrooms upstairs were hot in the summer, cold in the winter and thus seldom used.

In the downstairs bedroom, Mom and Dad's double bed set against one wall. Along the opposite wall under the window was my roll-away bed. A narrow walkway separated the beds.

Linda, my younger sister, and I were taking turns somersaulting from Mom and Dad's bed to mine. It was Linda's turn. She flipped from one bed to the other. Crash! Her foot smashed through the bottom window pane. Broken glass showered on her and the bed. Miraculously, she wasn't hurt. And, we weren't spanked. Dad took the broken window sash to town. He came home with it fixed as good as new.

After Dad replaced the sash, he turned to Linda and me. "Now girls," he said, "Let me show you how it's done." He took off his work shoes and stood in the middle of the double bed. As he shifted his weight the bed creaked under his 225 pounds,

1
Remember When...

five feet eight inches load.

Dad hiked up his faded bib overalls, ran his hand over his shiny bald head, then bent down and somersaulted across the walkway into my bed. Crash! His left foot smashed through the just-fixed window pane.

Dad slumped forward. His shoulders shook. Linda and I didn't know what to do. Was he hurt? No. He was laughing at himself so hard that he couldn't catch his breath.

One snowy day, Dad made us a sled out of old lumber. He used two 2 by 4's, four feet long for runners. "Come on girls, before we paint your new sled, let's go to that steep hill behind the corn crib and try it out."

Dad pulled the sled through the snow and we followed close behind. At the top of the hill he told us to "watch close. I'll go first and show you how it's done."

He backed up. With both hands he held the sled in front of him and took off in a dead run. He dropped the sled to the snow, then threw his bulky body on top. The sled disappeared into the snow. Dad slid down the hill on his nose. The result? Laughter, even though his nose was swollen for days.

Looking back to the 1940's and 1950's, home for us was a 290 acre farm in central Illinois about ten miles southwest of Sullivan, population 3,500. Farming was and is Dad's life. He has not lived anywhere other than on a farm, and has no desire to change. "When your roots are in the soil, they grow deep," he has always said.

Dad began farming on his own in 1941 with a new tractor, a two row corn planter, two row cultivator, two bottom plow, and a one row corn picker.

At the time, many farmers still used horses. Dad didn't. During one harvest season, it rained day after day. When Dad tried to pick his eighty acre cornfield behind the house, the tractor and corn picker settled into the deep mud. They were stuck there until the ground would freeze. Dad waited. But the rain didn't let up and the ground didn't freeze.

Finally, he borrowed his father's team of two work horses and hitched them to a steel wheeled wagon built up with three wooden sideboards. "Wilma," he said to Mother, "I'm going to shuck all that corn by hand." "I'll help," she replied. "Don't be silly, Wilma. You're too little. The mud will pull you down."

As he said that Mother raised to her full four feet

eleven inches, and squared all ninety-three pounds. Her brown eyes snapped. "I **will** help you," she insisted.

Dad shrugged his shoulders. "Suit yourself. But you won't last one round."

Mom lasted more than one round. She shucked corn all day as well as the next and the next, until all the corn was shucked and stored in the crib.

With loving care, Dad planted corn and soybeans in the spring, drilled wheat in the fall, and broadcasted clover seed when the clover field needed it. Throughout the year he plowed, disced, harrowed, hoed, and cultivated to help the grain "be fruitful and multiply."

Farming was and is one big gamble. Dad planted the grain on faith and hope. He prayed for rain at the right time, no hail at the wrong time, a late frost in the fall, and sunshiny summer days when he could almost see the corn grow.

He gave credit where credit was due. "God's been good to us. Don't forget to thank Him for all our blessings. But remember this: He expects us to do our share of the work."

Dad did more than his share of the work. He also did more than his share of worrying. He was strong on faith and hope but he somehow thought that worry and work went together. After he finished the work, he worried. What if he had not done all that he could?

Mom worried about one thing: how much Dad worried. She tried to calm him. "Don't worry about tomorrow," Mom would say, "God will take care of us." But, nothing helped if he was on a worrying spree. Finally, she threw up her hands in exasperation. "I quit worrying about you, Dale. You worry enough for both of us." And that's just what she did. Dad went on worrying and Mom let him.

Mom and Dad both grew up on farms. Their parents were thrifty, hard working farm folks. But that's where the similarity ended.

Mother was an only child. Her parents were afraid she would become too pampered and spoiled as an only child sometimes does. To save her from this fate, they supplied a ruled, disciplined life. Things were kept neat and in order. Proper table manners were practiced at every meal. No arguing was the rule. Quietness, neatness, and orderliness guided each day's routine.

Then she met Dad. He had five sisters and four brothers. Orderliness was not a rule in his home: Survival was. Two ways to settle an argument with a brother or sister were to yell louder and or hit harder. A house with ten children, two parents, and two grandparents was lived in from every angle. "Straightened" meant not colliding with anyone or anything during a mad dash for the door. The one table manner was "sit down, shut up, and eat before it's all gone."

As soon as we could toddle along, Linda and I helped Mom and Dad with the chores since our farm was a family affair. We all worked. Mom and Dad made the work fun. Linda and I tackled anything with self-confidence because Dad would say, "Go ahead, try it. I'll bet you can do it. Anyway, you'll never find out unless you try."

When we worked with Dad we moved fast. If he said, "Jump!", we jumped and asked, "How high?" on the way up. If he said, "Close that gate," we closed it. Even when we didn't know how or why.

Dad raised white-faced cattle. It was a Saturday morning in early spring when he said, "Nancy, come out and help me move the bull to the south pasture." I threw on my work jeans, denim waist coat, and dirty denim cap, then pulled up my black knee-high gum boots and tucked the blue jean legs inside the boots. Last came my work gloves. All donned in record time.

I dashed out the door and joined Dad in the backyard. "It's about time," he said. "We don't have all day. You stand at the top of the hill, I'll bring the bull around the barn and you head him toward the south pasture gate. Got that?"

"Got it," I said.

"Whatever you do, don't let the bull past you," Dad explained. "If he gets to the east pasture, it'll be days before we round him up again."

He disappeared behind the barn. Five minutes later, I hear thundering hooves. The big bull blasted around the corner of the barn. He was a massive hereford in rare form or feeling his oats you might say.

I planted my feet and spread my arms. The bull bore down on me. His huge horns measured at least four feet from tip to tip. I glared at him. He glared back. Without hesitation, I made my decision and stayed my ground. It was better to be run down by a bull than face Dad if I jumped out of the way and let the beast get by me.

I felt the bull's hot breath on my face. All at once, he put on his brakes, lost his balance, and rolled down the hill. The bull staggered to his feet than slowly strolled through the open gate into the south pasture.

Was Dad worried about me? Was he proud of my job well done? What did he say? "Close the pasture gate. Hurry!" I hurried.

With farm work, we were on twenty-four hour call, seven days a week. We never went on a vacation—we didn't all stay away from home overnight.

When visiting friends, Linda would say, "Can we stay longer?" "No," would be the answer. "Time to go home and milk the cows."

"Can we go to Chicago for a few days this week?" I would ask. "No, the cows are calving. We can't leave them now."

"May we go to the fair?" "Not yet. We have to get the hay in the barn before it rains."

"May we go to the fourth of July picnic?" "Not until we finish combining the wheat."

For years, I thought Dad knew everything and Mom knew nothing. If I asked Mom, "Can I go to Suzie's to play", she said, "Ask your Dad."

Or, "Why are there stars in the sky?" "Ask your Dad."

"May we go swimming?" "Ask your Dad."

"May I have a bicycle for my birthday?" "Ask your Dad."

Gradually, I began to learn how much Mom really knew. She knew Dad was a leader and wanted to feel in charge so she followed and Dad led—wherever Mom wanted him to go.

2

Home 'Sweet' Home

For ten years Mom and Dad maintained a rustic country home owned by Mom's dad, Grandpa Hogue. The only running water was at the well and cistern out back. And that water didn't run unless someone pumped the pump handles.

In arid summer weather, the cistern ran dry but a long cold drink of water flowed from the well after a good priming and rapid pumping. Winter or summer, day and night, a five gallon bucket of water, complete with dipper waiting to quench a thirst or wash the dirt, sat on the kitchen dry sink. On a winter night, ice formed over the water in the bucket.

Our house had three rooms downstairs and two slope-ceilinged rooms upstairs. There was no electric bill to pay because there was no electricity. Two gas lights lit our rooms at night; one light for the kitchen, and one for the front room.

One night when I was seven-years-old, Dad set the gas lamps out on the kitchen table. "Can I pump gas into the lamps?" I asked.

"Okay," said Dad. "Climb on a chair and start pumping." As I pumped, Dad turned the control valve, lit a match and held it under the lamp's white gauze filament. All of a sudden the lamp exploded, flames shot to the ceiling and escaping gas sprayed

onto the chair, the floor, and my new navy blue sailor dress. I jumped off the chair and darted for the front room.

As I ran by Mother, she grabbed at me, but missed. Dad leaped onto my back from behind. He crushed me between him and the floor. "Daddy! What are you doing?" I screamed.

"Lie still," he commanded. "The back of your dress is on fire, I'm smothering it out!" Meanwhile, Mom had transported the blazing lamp outside to the cistern pump and drowned the flames.

We survived with little damage: a scorched kitchen floor and a blackened back porch post where Mom ran by in her move to water. The back of my navy blue dress had been engulfed in flames: It wasn't even singed.

Soon after our gas light incident, Grandpa Hogue had the house wired for electricity.

A white metal Frigidaire replaced our brown wooden icebox in the kitchen and the iceman no longer came to our door with a block of ice clamped between iron-jaw carriers.

Naturally, our house didn't have a bathroom. An outhouse stood at the end of a crooked path thirty feet behind the house, next to the chicken house. The privy was an unpainted two seater. A sack of white lime leaned against the wall in one corner. From time to time, Mom or Dad tossed a shovelful of lime down each hole.

Late one afternoon I went into the house and called, "Mom?" She didn't answer. Outside, behind the house, I shouted for her again. Finally I heard her faint voice come from the outhouse. I darted down the path. The toilet door was latched from the inside. "Mom, are you in there?"

"Shhhh," she whispered. "Get your Dad."

"Why?" "Don't ask questions—Just do as I tell you," hissed Mom through the closed door.

I raced to the barn wondering why Mom wanted Dad in the toilet. "Daddy," I shouted. "Mom needs you. She's in the toilet." Dad dashed down the path with me close behind.

He rattled the toilet door. "Wilma, what's the matter?"

"There's a big blacksnake lying across the doorway. What'll I do?" she desperately whispered.

"Did you step over him when you went in?" asked Dad.

"Y-yes, I guess I did."

"Then step over him and come out," said Dad.

Carefully, Mom stepped out of the toilet. All the

way to the house Dad laughed and Mom growled, "Dale, you wouldn't think it was so funny if it had been you sitting there with a snake staring at you."

After that, I talked Linda into going to the toilet with me if I could find her in time. We'd open the door a crack to peek in at the floor and along the walls before entering. More than once we were almost too late, but we were never trapped in the toilet by a snake.

Old Sears and Roebuck catalogs ended up in our privy. They were recycled as toilet tissue long before we heard the word "recycling." The catalogs also served as "reading material while you wait." It was luxury when a roll of toilet tissue turned up in our outhouse even though there wasn't any reading on it.

One day I took some wooden matches, ran to the toilet, and latched the door from the inside. I tore off a long strip of white toilet tissue and rolled it as tight as possible. I put one end of the tissue "cigarette" between my lips and struck a match against the wall. An orange fire came to life. I held it under my "cigarette." Immediately, the tissue paper burst into flames. Before I could drop it from my mouth, the burning toilet tissue blistered the end of my nose.

Later at the supper table, Mom asked how I got the blister. "Did a bug bite you?" "Yeah, that's it." (A fire bug.)

It goes without saying, but I'll say it anyway. We didn't have a bathtub with hot and cold running water. Wednesday nights and Saturday nights were family bath nights. And I do mean family.

Dad carried in buckets of water from the cistern. While Mom warmed them on the kitchen stove, Dad took the oblong galvanized tub from its hook in the washhouse and set it behind the brown coal stove in the kitchen. When the water was warmed just right, Dad poured it into the tub then carried empty buckets out to the pump for more water.

Linda's bath was first. Being the youngest, she was the smallest which should have made her the cleanest. But sometimes she didn't look it. My turn came next. Same bath water. Same place. Mom's turn was third. She added a bucket of hot water to warm up the twice-used tepid bath. Dad was last. He added two more buckets of hot water from the stove and took a big bath for a big body. Afterwards, Mom and Dad carried out the tub between them and dumped the dirty water behind the washhouse.

Summer scrubbings came once a day in a

different way. Dad hammered nail holes in the bottom of a two gallon bucket and hung it from a hook between the washhouse and the storm cellar. When shower time arrived, Dad filled the holey bucket with rain water. We stood under the shower and scrubbed fast. It was a racing question: Would the water run out before the dirt ran off?

Linda was four-years-old and I was eight-years-old when we made our one and only childhood move. Our new home was one hundred yards up the road from our old home. It had three big rooms downstairs, three big rooms upstairs, and three big porches outside. Electricity was in; the bathroom was out. (Behind the chicken house again!) Grandpa Hogue owned this house, too. Dad farmed the same land as before. For seven more years we took bi-weekly baths behind the kitchen stove and made a well-worn path to the outhouse out back.

On a chilly morning, Dad carried in two buckets of red corn cobs; one for the kitchen stove and one for the front room stove. When the cobs were burning strong, he threw on black chunks of coal. That was our heating system. The twin stoves were square brown columns five feet tall with a pan of water on top. Four legs held each ugly stove off the floor. The square see-through door in front glowed red from the fire inside. Black stove pipes with an elbow bend carried smoke up the flue and out the chimney.

Mother raised Buff Orpington chickens; a buff colored breed of English origin eager to lay eggs as well as "finger-lickin' good to eat."

Early one freezing morning, Linda and I got out of bed and strolled into the front room. Behind the stove huddled twenty-five young buff orpington chicks in a makeshift pen of cardboard boxes. The smell of scorched chicken feathers filled the air and stung our nostrils. "What happened?" we asked.

"The chicken house burned last night," Mother replied. "The heat lamp exploded."

Linda and I ran to the window. Outside, flickering coals and charred lumber smouldered where a chicken house had stood the day before. "Where are all the other chickens?" I wanted to know.

Mom pointed to the sickly chicks behind the stove. "They're the only ones we saved—a hundred and fifty chickens burned."

That did it. Linda and I began to cry. Mother gathered us into her arms and consoled us. "Don't cry. We'll buy more chickens." Who wanted more chickens? We didn't even like them. Linda and I were crying because there had been a hot time in the chicken house last night and we had slept through it all!

Mom left the surviving chickens behind the front room stove until a temporary home was fixed for them in the garage later that day. Under normal conditions, she didn't allow animals in the house—not even our pet cats.

Somehow a cat often got into the house when Mom was outside in the garden or doing chores. Linda and I saw to the "Somehow." Trouble came when Mom returned to the house before we expected her. It wasn't easy to sneak a cat out of the house. If I squeezed him, he yeowled. If I stroked him, he purred. If I hid him under my shirt, his claws scratched my skin and I yeowled. No matter what, when, or how, Mom had a sixth sense that figured us out and found the cat.

Mother tried to keep us proper and in order. But it was three against one when it came to keeping our house neat and clean. On winter evenings, Dad stretched flat on his back in the middle of the front room floor. He supported Linda and me in flips flying the length of his body. With palms up, Dad extended his hands behind his head. Linda stood on Dad's hands. He raised her stiffened body up, up,

up until his arms were perpendicular to the floor. Forward rolls, backward rolls, and head stands graduated into forward flips, backbends, and hand stands. Dad, Linda and I performed nightly on the front room floor. Mother seldom practiced acrobatic stunts—she was too busy running after falling lamps and tobbling tables.

Mother's wringer washing machine was powered by a gasoline engine. Every Monday morning meant washday. Before breakfast, tubs of water boiled on the two burner gas stove in the washhouse behind our house. Into the washing machine went hot water and soap. Mom washed white clothes first, wrung them through the double rollers into luke-warm rinse water, then she wrung the same clothes through the rollers into a tub of cold rinse water. Once more, Mom guided the clothes through the wringer and squeezed out excess water.

She piled clean, wet clothes into a basket on our squeaky red wagon then pulled it to the clothesline in the chicken yard. Mom hung white clothes in the sun and colored clothes in the shade—unless Ted heard the wagon's squeak. .

Ted was our big brown dog, maybe part German shepherd, maybe not. Whatever he was, he learned tricks faster than any dog we ever had.

Linda and I taught Ted to shake hands, play dead, roll over, and jump through, over, or into anything. His first love was our red wagon. He would stop anything he was doing to ride in that wagon. Anytime he heard it's squeak, he leaped into it for a ride.

Monday was **not** the day for a wagon ride. Mom tied Ted to a tree and after loading the red wagon with two baskets of clean, wet clothes, she headed for the clothesline pulling the wagon behind her.

Time and again, Ted heard the squeak and went into action. He broke loose and darted around the house. If Mom saw him coming, she ran with wagon in tow: Ted ran faster. With a mighty leap, he would land on top of the wet clothes, tongue hanging and tail wagging. Mom yelled at him. She pleaded with him. She hit him. But nothing dampened Ted's love for the wagon ride. Not even the mud soaked clothes Mom had to re-wash.

Dad taught Linda and me how to maneuver machines almost before we could maneuver our own two feet. "Words can't teach you girls how to drive," said Dad. "It's experience behind the wheel that really counts."

I stood on the seat of Dad's blue 1939 Ford car and steered it down the road. Dad sat in the middle of the front seat and did the leg work: starting, stopping, and speeding. Mother rode with us. She didn't object. She couldn't. She was holding her breath in fear.

One day I was driving on the country road as usual. I was the ripe age of four. We turned a corner. Three cars were parked at the side of the road. Their drivers leaned against the middle car talking. Probably about the weather. Farmers do a lot of that. The three were our neighbors. Dad waved. I tried to wave. One small hand was left on the steering wheel.

The car swerved toward them. Men scattered. One tried to run but tripped and fell face first into the muddy ditch. A second neighbor took refuge on top of his car. The third man leaped onto the hood. We missed cars and people. Barely. Did Dad make me quit driving? No. I drove on down the road.

Dad laughed and laughed. "Did you see that,

3

Mechanical Maneuvers

Wilma? Sam dripping wet, Joe on top of his car, and Bill on the car hood. Fastest I've seen them move in a month."

Mom caught her breath. "It wasn't funny, Dale. Someone might have been hurt."

"It **was** funny," chuckled Dad. "I had control of the car. They just didn't know it." With that, even Mother had to muffle a smile.

Dad traded our old blue Ford for a new 1941 Ford (in 1943). It was shiny black and had four doors instead of two. The back two doors opened from the center post with hinges toward the back of the car. It's body design resembled an overgrown Volkswagen.

On separate occasions I smashed my left thumb, my right thumb, and my left index finger in the car's back doors. Each time my nail turned black and blue. Eventually it dropped off. Linda and I no doubt drove the black car, too but I don't remember. But I **do** remember how those back doors swung.

Dad always said, "You can tell a man's worth by how he keeps his car." If Dad said it, that was the way it was; as far as we were concerned. Regularly, the four of us washed, waxed, and polished the car. It didn't matter how old the paint was, elbow grease made our car shine. Nobody

looked at our car and said, "There goes a worthless man."

Dad demanded two things of his car engine: speed and a smooth sound. Fast was the only way he drove. When we went anywhere, we got there in a hurry. He was a good driver. He didn't want one of his cars marred by a scratch or dent. That's why he outran everything else on the road.

I had just turned sixteen when I backed our 1957 Ford into a woven wire fence and scraped a fin.

I drove home, got out of the car, sat down on the ground and cried. Dad rushed out of the garage. "What happened?"

"Scratched the car," I wailed. "Back there. On the fin."

Dad looked the car over. "I don't see anything except where my overall snaps rubbed. I squeezed in between the car's fin and the garage wall yesterday." I started to open my mouth. Yesterday had been Sunday. He had worn a suit when he drove the car to church. I cried louder.

"Now what?" asked Dad. "Don't cry. Everything's all right." I shook my head. Dad's car was scratched. I had done it. He knew it. And I knew he knew. Yet, he told me a little white lie because my feelings meant more to him than any machine.

That was one reason why we all jumped when Dad said, "Jump!" He would do the same and more for us.

Minor accidents came easy for me. I learned fast how to scrape and scratch. Mom and Dad gave me a new blue bicycle when I was seven. It was a mechanical device I learned to maneuver in one day. The following day it was 'tricky' how I maneuvered my new bicycle into the tailgate of a neighbor's pickup truck. No one told me my new bike had brakes!

I was eight when I said I was going to ride my bike to Aunt Elsie's. "You can't today," said Dad. "Road graders tore up the road yesterday. Last night's rain made it too muddy for bike riding."

"I can ride my bike on it. Mud won't bother me."

"It'll stick to your tires until they won't turn under the bicycle fenders."

"It won't either," I insisted. "Anyway, if I get mud on my tires, I'll just stop and scrape it off."

"Go ahead," said Dad. "But you'll have trouble."

I went ahead. I had trouble. Mud built up on my tires until the wheels wouldn't turn beneath the bicycle fenders. I scraped off the mud. In no time, it was caked on again. There I was, half way between going and coming, caught in the middle of a mud sea without a bike to pedal.

I looked up. Dad was driving the truck toward me. "Old Hoopie" slid about in the muddy road. Without a word of "I told you so," Dad waded through the mud, picked up my messy bike and laid it in the back of the truck. In the truck cab, I huddled against the opposite door. Dad climbed in behind the wheel. He drove to a field culvert and turned the truck around. We slid home through the mud in silence. No words were necessary. I'd learned my lesson the hard way again. I should have listened to Dad. He knew what he was talking about.

Dad had bought his first truck in 1950. Right away, he named the rattling green Ford "Old Hoopie." Linda and I loved to ride in the back of the truck and let the wind tangle our hair.

One day Old Hoopie almost became a convertible. Dad was driving alone when he came up on county road work trucks; one on either side of the road. He slowed the truck. No flagmen or warning signs were in sight so Dad decided to drive on. A cable stretched across the road smashed into Hoopie's windshield shattering it. Glass flew everywhere. Dad slammed on his brakes. But not quite soon enough. Hoopie was permanently damaged.

15

The road workers were at fault. They paid to repair the truck. The frame was bent back into place; a new windshield installed. From then on, if the wind blew, Hoopie shook. If it rained, Hoopie leaked.

I was twelve when I first soloed in the yellow and green truck that replaced Hoopie. Linda rode with me. We drove around and around in the clover field south of the house. It was good training, I think. I don't know about my sister, but I've gone around in circles ever since.

Trucks and cars weren't all we drove at an early age. Tractors were part of our training, too. Linda and I were outside helping Dad haul manure out of the barn. She was three. I was seven. Dad hooked the manure spreader behind the tractor. He drove the tractor to the barn and parked the spreader beneath an open window. I followed Dad into the barn to watch him pitch manure out the window into the spreader. Linda stayed outside. Several minutes passed.

All at once the tractor started up. The manure spreader sped away from the window. Dad and I dashed out of the barn door in time to see Linda shut off the tractor fifty yards away. Linda merely shrugged her narrow shoulders and said, "I wanted

to see if I could drive it."

Dad bought old Allis when I was twelve. It was a used orange Allis Chalmers tractor, very used. My specialty was discing with Allis. As the tractor hummed or sputtered across the field I sang all the songs I knew at the top of my voice. Neighbors looked my way. People passing in cars slowed and stared. I felt proud. They were amazed that a girl

my age could do such a good job farming. How was I to know they heard my singing above the tractor's roar and thought I was calling for help?

No neighbors or travelers need worry when I plowed. I didn't feel like singing then. It took too much of my concentration to keep one big wheel in the furrow, make the furrow straight, and trip the two bottom plow at each end of the field.

One morning, I hoed rows of tender young soybeans. Actually, I massacred them. A rock caught in the tractor hoe and I didn't look back until two half-mile rows of soybeans were forever gone. Boy, did I hate to tell Dad. But I had to. How could I hide a big bare space in the bean field all summer? He surveyed the destruction, then handed me a bag of seed beans, and said, "Start plantin'."

Linda took her turn behind the wheel in the field on the Allis Chalmers tractor. Although she was a tiny ten-years-old, she did a good job of discing—if Dad could keep her on the tractor. You see, she disced pass her friend June's house on the way around the field. If June was outside, Linda stopped the tractor, left it in the field with the engine idling, and played with June.

After a couple of years, Dad traded Allis for an International M tractor. I loved that tractor.

Gripping its steering wheel, I felt the potential power at my finger tips.

One afternoon in the hayfield two miles south of our house, Dad said, "Take the tractor home, Nancy."

"In what gear?" I asked.

"Drive it in any gear you think you can handle."

I wheeled the tractor home in high gear, full throddle, wide open. Mother ran out of the house and met me in the driveway. "What do you think you're doing, Nancy? Speeding like that. You might have been killed!"

Before I could answer, Dad drove in on the H tractor. Mother ran to him. "Dale, did you see Nancy?"

"Sure did. I told her to drive in a gear she could handle. Reckon she handled it." Mother threw up her hands and stomped back to the house.

Linda and I drove the tractor during daylight hours. It wasn't work to us. It was fun. It was a game. Dad didn't stop working when the sun went down. If it was time to plant and the weather was right, he drove on into the night.

For a farmer there is a time to reap and a time to sow; a time to rest, and a time to **go**—before the rain comes.

4

Growing With God

Mother and Dad knew God. They recognized God's loving presence and thanked Him for life's ups and downs.

After we girls were born, it became easier to go to the Bruce Methodist church. Bruce, a village of forty-seven people, two small groceries, one blacksmith shop, a two room school, and one church was three miles east of our farmhouse. Windsor was seven miles south. With all the morning chores, closer was best. We ran a better chance of arriving on time. Sunday or not, the chores had to be done first.

Grandma Hogue attended the church in Windsor. She was raised in a strict religious family. Card playing was evil. No one sewed or cleaned on Sunday. Any game using dice was frowned upon. Grandma cooked most of Sunday's dinner on Saturday because the Sabbath was a day of rest.

Dad didn't share her views so Grandma relaxed her strict standards a bit. Still, she worried about Linda and me. Would we, her only grandchildren, outgrow the tomboy stage and finally become ladies?

One day, Grandma and I were walking in the pasture. I spotted the cattle nearby. "Grandma, see our new bull."

"Oh, Nancy, " she said. "That's not my little girl. You must say Mr. Cow."

At Bruce, Sunday School was held every Sunday. Church services took place twice a month. Our minister divided his time between two tiny churches. His other Methodist congregation was in Allenville, six miles east of Bruce. One Sunday he preached at Allenville; the next Sunday at Bruce. Did he preach the same sermon two Sundays in a row? If so, which congregation was the better listener?

I didn't ask our minister questions. He was big. And the way he shouted and pounded his fists in the pulpit every other Sunday morning kept me worried as well as awake.

Our white clapboard church's twenty-seven people half-filled the pews. Mom played the piano during church and taught children in the dark damp basement during Sunday School.

A faded pink curtain separated my class from the older children's class. A little kid can learn a lot listening to the big kids on the other side of a curtain in Sunday School: like who's going with whom, or who shared blankets at the free show in the pasture Thursday night.

In the Methodist church people were baptized by sprinkling or submersion. The choice was up to the individual. Four people requested submersion. Bruce church had no baptistry. On a dry, hot Sunday in August, we attended the baptismal service.

Dad drove Mom, Linda, and me to the Stricklan Bridge two miles northeast of Bruce. Instead of crossing the bridge, he turned down a dirt road beside the Kaskaskia River. Dust filled the air. No cars were visible ahead or behind. Sandy dust clouds told us they were there. At last, Dad stopped the car. Walking on sandy, clay-packed ground we joined other congregation members on the river bank.

Two men and two women waited to be baptized. They stood with the minister at the water's edge. The three men wore white shirts open at the neck and dark wash pants. Their feet were bare. The women wore long white robes.

One by one, Reverand Starwaldt led them into the river's languid water. He baptized them in the name of the Father, the Son, and the Holy Ghost.

Waterlogged new church members waded out reborn of God under blue cloudless skies. Everyone sang "Shall we gather at the river that flows by the grace of God." What an imprint the service left on my seven-year-old mind!

Five years later, Bruce church lost its part-time minister. We began attending the First Christian Church in Sullivan. Two hundred people filled the pews every Sunday.

On January 1, Linda and I stepped forward and made our confessions of faith. At the same time, Mom and Dad transferred their memberships from Windsor to Sullivan.

Two weeks later, the minister held the baptismal service. Linda and I were to be submerged in the baptistry behind the pulpit. "Each of you will carry a folded white handkerchief in your left hand," the minister told us. "Just before I baptize you, I'll take the handkerchiefs from you and place it over your mouth and nose. I'll have an extra white hand-kerchief in my breast pocket in case one of yours gets wet," he added. How silly, I thought. In just three feet of water anybody can keep a folded handkerchief dry.

Linda was baptized first. She kept her hand-kerchief dry. My turn came. I stepped down into the water. My full white robe hit the water and fanned out from my body. With both hands, I shoved it against me. The minister calmly took the dry white handkerchief from his breast pocket and laid it over my mouth and nose. I was baptized with one wet handkerchief clutched in my left hand.

Music held deep meaning in the worship services. Dad's favorite hymns were "In the Garden," "The Old Rugged Cross," and "When the Roll is Called up Yonder." In addition to Dad's favorites, Mom loved to play and sing "Beulah Land" and "Will There be any Stars in my Crown".

"Nancy, you sang in church when you were two years old," Dad told me.

"I could sing hymns then?" I asked in amazement.

"Well—not exactly. Everyone else was singing "Sweet Hour of Prayer." You sang "Bell Bottom Trousers'."

"Was I loud?"

"Very."

"Did you do anything about it?" At that point Mother interrupted our conversation. "Yes, your Dad laughed. I covered your mouth."

I was surprised to learn that Mom didn't practice her infamous "pinch in public." I guess it came later.

If Linda and I talked in church, Mom casually laid her hand on our legs. She pinched us hard. It had to be our little secret. If Linda or I yelled "Ouch," a peach limb licking greeted us at home. We under-

20

stood Mom's silent message fast—and often.

Mom's favorite "learning rod" was the limber peach limb. A limitless supply hung in the peach tree outside our back door. Mom laid the limbs on top of the refrigerator in easy reach. I hid one limb after another. She didn't bother to search for them. For when I needed a spanking, she stepped outside and cut another limb off the tree.

Linda spent her punishment time sitting on a kitchen chair. Chair sitting hit her where it hurt better than peach limbs. In a crowd or at church our punishment was equally the same: Mom's silent pinch.

Back when Linda was five and I was nine, an evangelist held a week of nightly revival meetings in our country church. He preached hellfire and damnation at a frenzied pitch. He needed no microphone to be heard. By the end of the sermon, his voice grew hoarse. Singing voices were louder than they had ever been before. Strangers filled the pews. Each night one or two soles went forward and made their confessions to God before men.

At the close of the third night of revivals a tall, shapely woman in a tight fitting bright blue dress walked up the aisle. Her jet black hair was piled high on her head. She had ebony arched eyebrows and thick lashes. Her lips were scarlet. Circles of rouge reddened her cheeks.

She knelt before the altar. Again and again, the evangelist asked her, "Do you feel the cleansing spirit of God?"

Each time she shook her head.

After what seemed hours she threw up her arms and screamed, "Oh, dear God. I feel it. I feel it!"

Few eyes were dry as the congregation sang the closing hymn "Blest be the ties that bind our Hearts in Christian love."

The woman came every night after that. I watched closely for any change in her appearance. Every night she looked the same as the first time I saw her. I was puzzled. "Mom, why does that woman still wear tight clothes and lots of make-up if she believes in God?"

"It's how she feels about God inside that counts, not what she wears. Accept her as she is, God does," said Mother.

"Then can I wear a lot of makeup?" I asked.

"No. What's right for one person may be wrong for another. Besides, you're too young."

Needless to say, I was still puzzled.

Mother encouraged prayer. I prayed about everything. "Dear God, please let there be a letter in the mailbox for me. Amen." There was no letter in the mailbox for me.

"Dear God, please let me get an A on my math test today. Amen." No A. I didn't study.

"Dear God, please let me get the lead part singing in the operetta. Amen." No lead part. I couldn't sing.

"Dear God, please let Joe like me. Amen." No Joe. He didn't even know my name.

God was supposed to answer all prayers. Why wasn't He listening to me? Finally, I took my questions to Mom. "Why didn't God answer my prayers?"

"God did answer your prayers. He said 'No.' Maybe if you had studied you would have deserved an A on the math test. Or, if you wrote a letter, there'd be an answer in the mailbox. Try asking God what He wants you to do, not what you want Him to do for you."

As a growing child, I prayed to the picture of Jesus. When I closed my eyes for meditation an artist's drawing of Jesus was what my mind saw. "Mom, I see pictures of Jesus. What does God look like?"

"God is a spirit," said Mom.

"Isn't He a big man with a long white beard that sits on a gold throne in heaven?" I asked.

"He has no face," said Mom.

"At Sunday School we read in the first chapter of Genesis that God created man in His own image. Don't we look like God?"

"We're created in the spiritual image of God, Nancy. We think, choose, and have eternal souls if we live right."

I had to continue growing physically and spiritually before I began to understand what Mother was trying to tell me.

Then I heard the words: There is no God. I ran to Mother. "Is that true?"

"Is the earth round?" asked Mother.

"Yes."

"How do your know?"

"I read it in my science book at school. I can see the earth's shadow on the moon. And I can see a curve in the horizen."

"You haven't seen the earth's sphere yet you believe in its shape," said Mother. "I haven't seen God but I know He's here with us. I've read His words in the Bible. I've seen His work in a flower, a field of wheat, and a baby's face. The miracles of God-given life and love are all around us."

Mom's explanation made sense to me. My faith in

God grew stronger.

Number seven of the ten commandments began to worry me. I understand the commandments to worship one God, worship no images, never break oaths, rest on Sunday, honor my parents, and to not kill, lie, steal, or be jealous. But what did "Thou shalt not commit adultery" mean?

I asked Mother. "Wait until you're thirteen," she said.

I asked Dad. "Wait until you're thirteen," he said.

I didn't want to wait. I wanted to know then. I went to the Webster's Dictionary. Adultery meant voluntary sexual intercourse by a married man with another than his wife or by a married woman with another than her husband. So, that was adultery. But—what was sexual intercourse? Back to the dictionary I went. Sexual meant associated with being male or female. Intercourse was dealings between persons, organizations, or nations as in business: communication.

There was my answer. Adultery meant voluntary association between a man and a woman other than his wife or her husband in business, national or organizational dealings. Communication was a letter or telephone call between opposite sexes.

Why would God forbid that 4000 years ago?

"Am I right, Mother?" "No. Wait until you're thirteen."

By and by, I became 13. Mother and Dad took me aside and told all. Boy, did Mr. Webster and his dictionary lead me astray!

The threat of tornadoes terrified me. One might kill me. I wasn't ready to die. My whole life was ahead of me. What could I do if a tornado came our way? Where would I go to be safe? When the wind blew stronger than a gentle breeze, I knew a tornado had to be on the way.

One stormy night, I cried and cried. Finally, I confessed my fears to Dad. "I'm afraid. We'll be blown away. We're going to die."

"No one knows how long he has on this earth. But living in constant fear is no way to spend the life God gave you," said Dad. "Have you seen any tornadoes lately?"

"N-no."

"Neither have I. Stop worryin' till you see one."

Two weeks later, I read in the paper "World Ends October 15, 1953." The end was coming. By fire, of course. The Bible said the heavens and earth would be destroyed by fire. Somehow a newspaperman had an inside story as to when the fire would begin to destroy the world. I had ten days to live. Eight days crawled by. I fretted in silence every waking moment.

At dusk on the eighth day a strange redness flickered in the northern sky. Had the fire started two days ahead of schedule? "W-what's that," I asked Dad as I pointed to the sky.

"Look at it," said Dad. "Wilma, come here. It's northern lights. You don't see them often. It's caused by elements of the sun glowing in our atmosphere. Isn't it beautiful?"

"I thought the end of the world had come two days early," I told him.

"You read that in the paper, didn't you?"

"Yes. And the Bible says the world will be destroyed by fire."

"Read more of the Bible. You'll find that there's no way for any of us to know when the end of the world will come. Don't worry about it. Worry over things you can do something about. That's in the Bible, too. Isn't it, Wilma?"

She had joined us while Dad was talking. "Yes," she said. "It's in the sixth chapter of Matthew, thirty-fourth verse. "so, do not worry about tomorrow; it will have enough worries of its own. There is no need to add to the troubles each day brings." Mother paused then looked straight at Dad and added, "That's what I gave up trying to tell you, Dale."

Dad didn't say anything. He shoved his hands into the side pockets of his faded overalls and watched the radiant aurora borealis.

When Mom and Dad were married, Dad's parents gave them a Jersey heifer for a wedding gift. As the years went by, Jerse mothered Jersey-holstein-hereford calves. They in turn mothered half jersey-holstein-hereford and half hereford calves. The herd grew until it averaged thirty dual purpose, white-faced cows, dominated by a succesion of hereford bulls (with one holstein bull thrown in along the way). Some cows were milked, others were sold as beef cattle.

Mom and Dad's Jerse was mother, grandmother, great grandmother, and on, and on, to all the cattle. The only strangers to the herd's family tree was a new bull every two years.

What would Linda and I have done without cows for playmates? Our imagination and energy ran wild as cowgirls capering among the cows. Think of it. Would Jack have had a beanstalk if he hadn't first had a cow?

If it hadn't been for the cows, who would have been in the corn to hear Little Boy Blue blow his horn?

And if the cow hadn't jumped over the moon, what would the little dog have had to laugh about?

Who would have started the great Chicago fire in 1871 if Mrs. O'Leary's cow hadn't kicked over a

5 Cowgirl's Capers

lantern that fateful night in October?

If it hadn't been for the cows of our youth, Linda and I would've had a lot of time to kill and few tales to tell.

Milking the cows by hand was a family affair. Twice a day, Dad milked four, Mom milked two, I milked one and one-half, and Linda milked one-half. Dad's fast pull finished off our two 'one-halfs.'

One of the one and one-half cows I milked was Daisy, a big black cow more holstein than hereford. On a hot summer evening, flies swarmed in the milkshed pestering the cows. Balanced on a one-legged stool with the milk bucket between my knees, I squeezed Daisy's handles. Milk foamed in the bucket. Daisy's tail slapped at the flies on her back. Her aim was off. Again, and again, her heavy tail pounded across the back of my neck. Finally, I tucked Daisy's tail behind my bent knee and held it there. It stopped her tail lapping but it didn't stop the flies crawling along her body.

She kicked. I blocked the kick with my left arm. She kicked again. I wasn't so lucky. Her hoof scraped across my nose, cheek, hit my collarbone, and landed in my bucket of milk. I crashed to the floor. Spilt milk soaked my clothes. Muddy manure covered my face. "Dad, help," I yelled.

He stepped around behind Daisy. There I was sprawled on the floor in a pool of milk. Did he worry about me? No. Did he help me up? No. He laughed—and laughed—and laughed. The cow's kick didn't hurt me but Dad's laughter did. My self-esteem was cracked. I quit—until the next morning.

Spilt milk was my specialty. I would leave the milkshed with two buckets of milk and arrive at the house with nothing but empty buckets and muddy milk stains. Along the way, I tripped over cats, twigs, tree roots, or my own two feet.

Those falls meant less milk for the ten gallon cans Dad set in the driveway each morning for the milkman to pick up and take to the cheese factory in town.

The weekly milk check was divided among the milkers minus Dad. For example, if the milk check was $26.48, Mom got $25.00 and we sisters divided $1.48 for our piggy banks. My clumsiness shrank our milk check at the end of the week. We all suffered from my awkward falls.

In 1958, Dad slipped a disc in his lower back. He was ordered to bed. Mom, Linda, and I, with the help of a neighbor, milked and fed the cattle.

Dad remained flat of his back for three more

weeks. By and by, Linda and I got tired of toiling and the good neighbor had other things to do. Mother couldn't feed twenty-two head of cattle and milk eight others twice a day alone. One morning she let the calves have all their mothers' milk, not just the leftovers.

Dad's era of dual purpose cattle in wooden milking stanchions ended. The time of all-beef cattle at the feed troughs began. Same cattle; different goals. We never again led Jerse, Blackie, Daisy, Martha, Mary, Spot, Brentle, and Betty into the milkshed.

We no longer hooked their heads in stanchions, took the one-legged stool off the hook, sat on it beside a cow, and swished milk into buckets to the rhythm of crunching corn and breathing cattle with smells of wild onion, sweat, manure, and sweet clover hay.

Store-bought milk didn't taste the same as home-pasteurized milk. Thank goodness. No green onion taste, no hedge apple taste.

Our poor cats suffered the most. Before the shutdown they circled the feet of milk givers and milk getters meowing for a stream of warm milk squirted in their faces straight from the "factory."

When Linda was six and I was ten, Dad said, "Girls, pick out a calf and we'll be partners. From now on half of her and her calves will be yours and half will be mine."

Linda chose a golden brown calf with brown markings on its white face and named her Alyce Faye. I selected a white faced hereford calf and named her Princess Ann. We spent long, patient hours teaching Princess Ann and Alyce Faye to follow our rope halter leads.

At six month, Princess Ann weighed six hundred pounds. One day, I led her around the barn lot as my mind dwelled on wishes for horses. Years earlier, Dad had diagnosed my wishing ailment. "You've got the epizudic," he said. "What's that?" I had asked. "Wants for a horse." If that was the epizudic, I had it bad.

Why not train Princess to be my "horse?" I would ride her everywhere. Resting my right leg across her back, I inched up, up, and over until I straddled her bony backbone. She didn't move. I nudged her side with the heel of my gum boot and said, "Git up, Princess." She did. I rode as she walked about the barn lot.

Many hours of riding Princess followed. When she trotted, I grasped the halter rope and held on with my knees clamped like a vice against her broad ribs. It was a rough ride but it was the next best thing to having a horse. Or was it?

Princess didn't respond to rein guidance. Therefore, I had little control over our destination. We got along fine unless she didn't want to go in the direction I pulled her head.

One temperamental afternoon, she trotted to a barbed wire fence and scraped her side against the sharp barbs. Her body pinned my right leg between her and the fence. I moved fast, but not fast enough. A wire barb tore through my jeans and cut a six inch gash down my right leg.

After that episode, if Princess headed for a fence, I immediately threw the threatened leg across her back and rode sidesaddle.

On another afternoon, Linda and I were riding double. Princess grew tired of the extra weight so she laid down on a feed trough in the middle of the feed lot. Linda and I jumped clear just in time. The flattened feed trough wasn't as fortunate.

Nothing dampened our enthusiasm. The next day, Linda and I rode double again. This time we were in the rolling pasture behind the barn. I climbed off. "Do you want to get down and hold Princess's rope, Linda?"

"No. I'll stay on her back and hold the rope," said Linda.

I left them on the hill top for a few minutes. When I returned, they were nowhere in sight. No cow. No Linda. "Where are you?" I yelled.

"Nancy! Get me loose," Linda's faint voice came from the bottom of the hill. I ran down the slope. Linda lay flat on her back under the cow. Her long blonde hair was pinned to the ground beneath Princess's hind hoof. That cow knew she had Linda trapped. What's more, she enjoyed it.

A salesman came to see Dad. They stood in the driveway and talked. The salesman faced the barnyard. Dad's back was to it.

"Hello, I'm Don Green. I want to talk to you about—about—what's that?"

"What's what?" asked Dad.

"Nothing. As I was saying, I'm representing a new brand of hybred seed corn and—there they go again. Turn around, Mr. Lane. Look! It's two kids riding double around and around the barn on a **cow**."

"Sure. That's my girls. They do it all the time."

Seed corn selling was forgotten. Mr. Green and Dad leaned on the barnyard fence and watched us ride Princess Ann. "I must bring my kids to see this," said Mr. Green.

After a year's experience of riding my cow, I learned the secret for speed from Princess. I led her up the drive and down the road as far from the barn as I dared. Then I turned her around and climbed onto her back. We were off. She gave me the fastest, bumpiest one way trip to the barn everytime.

As Princess Ann grew older, she became more temperamental. One morning, I offered her an ear of corn. Instead of taking the corn with gratitude, she pawed the ground with her left front hoof, let out a bellow, and charged! I rammed the car of corn down her throat as far as my arm could reach. She stopped—but not until my arm was in her mouth up to the elbow. It didn't take long for me to interpret her message. I left her completely alone that day and any other day she felt like fighting.

I was always dense when it came to learning from experiences. (I heard that somewhere before.) I experienced and experienced but seldom learned.

Dad and I watched the cattle drinking from the water tank in the feed lot. I spotted a sleek yearling bull. "I bet I can ride him" I said.

"Better not," said Dad. "He's big and he's never had anyone on his back."

"I can ride him," I said. "Watch."

Dad didn't argue with me. As usual he left it to me to discover the truth.

The bull stood against a white board fence. I climbed to the top board and eased my body off the fence onto his back. Nothing happened. He didn't stop drinking water. I gave Dad a triumphant grin.

All at once, that bull bucked—and bucked! I hung on because I didn't know how to get off a whirling tornado. Each time his feet hit the ground, my teeth felt as if they were torn out by the roots. The bull twisted beneath me. My body flew through the air. I slammed into the concrete foundation of the feed barn. Stars swirled in blackness before my eyes. I felt as if I'd never breathe again.

Soon the roaring in my ears was replaced by Dad's laughter. He laughed so hard he couldn't catch his breath. Eventually, he helped me to my feet. "Here I am dying," I gasped, "and all you can do is laugh." Luckily the only thing hurt was my pride. I must admit, I didn't try to ride that bull any more. I left him completely alone.

"I wish I could ride Alyce Faye like you ride Princess," said Linda.

"I'll break her to ride for you," I said.

Linda led her cow into a small triangular corral on the east side of the milkshed. Alyce Faye was a

smaller animal than Princess. They were the same age but Alyce Faye had taken after her Jersey ancestry whereas Princess was more holstein-hereford.

With little effort, I jumped astride Alyce Faye's back and waited. She didn't move anything but her head. It inched lower and lower to the ground. I waited ten minutes. Still she didn't move. Linda watched from her seat on the corral fence. Dad stood beside her whittling on the top fence board.

"Okay, Linda," I said. "You try her now. Nothing to it."

All at once the cow shot straight up, came down, and took off. I was thrown to the ground with such force that my boots flew off. Guess who laughed until he couldn't catch his breath. Dad, of course.

I looked up at Linda and said, "Boy, was I wrong. She wasn't broke after all."

Linda was mad. "It wasn't your fault, Nancy. See Dad's knife? He stuck her."

Linda and I passed many a day playing games sisters play. The names of our favorite games were Amuse, Annoy, and Argue. Our rules were tease, aggravate, and pester one another.

I was four years older; Linda was four speeds faster. Dad said, "Linda **HAD** to learn to run faster. If Nancy ever caught up with her, she was sure to loose the fight."

Curled up in a front room chair, I began reading a good book. Linda strolled by. She shoved my elbow. I ignored her. Retracing her steps, Linda grabbed the book from my hands. She slammed it shut, dropped it into my lap, and ran.

Once more, I ignored her as I looked for my place in the book. Linda darted by, yanked the book from my hands, and sped away. I took off after her. The chase was on. We ran through the bedroom, around the kitchen table, out the back door, across the porch, around the house, and in the front door to start the circle all over again.

Some mornings, before getting out of bed, I said to myself, "I'm going to pester the heck out of Linda today." And that's what I did. When passing her chair I pulled her hair. I hid her comb around the house. I rode her bike out of sight. I didn't play anything her way. It was my duty to get in the last

6

Games Sisters Play

word—and the last hit.

On congenial days, we played "house" outside. Linda swept a patch of dirt clean. I laid wall boundaries of sticks and stones. We stirred up mud pies, packed sand cakes, and baked rock rolls for dinner. Dissolved soap chips made mimic milk and sudsy soup. Our floor table was set with shells, cottonwood leaves, and treasures from the trash pile.

Linda and I played game after game of croquet. First we argued over who got red because red went first. If enough daylight time was left after our arguing, we played the game.

Emma Lou came to play croquet. She lived a mile down the road and was three years older than I (seven years older than Linda). Emma Lou took the red mallet and ball. She went first. She took Linda's Snicker candy bar. She took over. "Does shrimp-o have to play with us?" asked Emma Lou. "Yes," I said. "Linda has to play."

Emma Lou played out of turn ahead of Linda. Next time around, Linda hit Emma Lou's red ball with her green one. "You can't do that. You're dead on me," said Emma Lou.

"No, I'm not," said Linda. "I'm going to send your ball."

Emma Lou strutted over to Linda. "You can't do it. Don't touch my ball."

Linda swung back to hit her ball. The croquet mallet smashed into Emma Lou's nose.

"My nose. My nose," howled Emma Lou. "It's all Linda's fault. She hit me on purpose. I'm tellin'."

Linda and I glared at Emma Lou. Together we said, "Go home." Emma Lou took off down the road. She took along a fat, red nose. Sisters may pick on each other, but no one may pick on one's sister.

By and by, badminton replaced croquet as our favorite outdoor play on a summer day. Linda's badminton racket swing didn't carry quite the force of her croquet mallet.

Linda and I were teenagers when we began playing softball on the girls' traveling team in Sullivan. Our summer days were then filled with practice, practice, practice. We gave each other a softball fundamental workout all over the front yard. Tired was not a word in our vocabulary.

We warmed up with a session of pitch and catch. The policy was to pitch with all our might and always catch it right. The more it stung the hand in our gloves the better. Next came ball grounders back and forth. We stopped them fast then fired them back with a blast. At fly ball practice we caught three batted flies to win a batting turn. Can "practice makes perfect" be true? We practiced and practiced but we never did make perfect.

Most of our toys were homemade. Dad made us each a pair of stilts. He laid two, 1 by 2 inch boards side by side and cut each at the length of six feet. Fourteen inches from the end, he nailed a one inch thick chunk of wood four inches square onto each long board.

Linda and I walked on stilts day after day. We had great fun being eighteen inches taller than usual. We learned to stilt walk across our mole-maize front yard. Ultimately, we mastered step climbing on stilts.

Another game of balance was barrel walking. We laid a metal oil drum about two feet in diameter on its side. Linda stood on it. With bare feet, she rolled the barrel forward and backward around the house.

Trouble came when Linda and I tried walking the barrel together. Four bare feet on one barrel didn't move in the same direction at the same time. It was a bit painful for the fannies when a barrel flipped us off backwards onto hard rocks and dirt.

Dad bought a long rope as big around as his wrist.

He tied one end to a tree branch thirty feet above the ground. On the other end he tied a rubber tire. Linda and I flew back and forth in our rubber tire swing faster and farther than anyone else. It hung in the chicken yard for twenty years. And then, one day, a part of our childhood was cut away.

"Girls need strong muscles, too," Dad had said. He suspended an iron bar on two ropes tied to a tree limb. The trapeze bar hung six feet above the ground. Every day Linda and I tried more difficult stunts as we competed against each other on our trapeze swings.

Swinging from both knees was simple for Linda and me. One knee swinging was not. Sitting on the bar was easy. Swinging from one heel wasn't; we tried it again and again but failed. To hang over the bar by the stomach was no problem. To hang over the bar by the back was painful.

Linda and I traveled the country roads by piggy-back biking. I furnished the pedal power and the bicycle. Linda had the holding power until she was old enough to power her own pedals. Riding on the carrier over my bike's back fender, she kept her feet out of the spokes and leaned into every turn.

"Make Believe" was the game we played in the ninety-three acre timber pasture behind our house.

Linda and I ran barefooted up and down the cow paths through the woods. In creeks, we waded downstream and looked for tadpoles. We splashed upstream and found a cave. (It was actually a gully dug out by rushing water.) A tree had fallen across the top. Our branch roof blocked out the sun. The cave was cool. And it was our secret. We spent long summer days hiding in our cave from Indians and wild animals.

When we grew tired of hiding, Linda and I lay on a grassy hillside and watched clouds roll by in the summer sky. "I see a lamb." "There's the hand of God." "Look over there, that cloud looks like cotton. I wish I could reach up and touch it."

"If wishes were horses, then beggars would ride." "Wish I had a horse," I said. "Wish I had a horse too," said Linda.

Dad had two saw horses made from a horizontal board held up by four wooden legs. On our stationary stallions, Linda and I "rode" to our dream world of cowboys and Indians, princesses and knights, or law men and outlaw men. Still, we wished for a real live horse.

We wished on the first star at night. We wished on chicken wishbones. We wished on white horses—even the neighbor's dirty white mule.

Finally, something worked because we got our wish.

Linda was three and I was seven when Dad said, "I talked to Sam today. He has a skinny little sorrel mare that he says is as gentle as a kitten." We wanted her sight unseen. Dad went to vist Sam the next day. He came home with the prettiest skinny horse Linda and I had ever seen. "What's her name?" asked Linda.

"That's up to you girls," said Dad. When I was growing up, we had a horse that looked like this one. Her name was Lulabelle."

We named our new horse Lulabelle. Right away, we started stuffing her with oats and molasses. Within three weeks she filled out and felt her oats.

Linda sat in the saddle on Lulabelle's back. She dangled her feet. They couldn't reach the stirrups. Linda rode halfway around the yard. Lulabelle laid down. Linda hopped off just in time. Our "Gentle" horse rolled over with the saddle under her. If Linda's feet had been in the stirrups, Lulabelle's body would have crushed her.

The next day, I rode Lulabelle into the pasture. Without warning, she swung around and galloped to the hedge row fence at the far end of the pasture. I gripped the saddle horn with one hand and yanked at the reins with the other. She paid no attention as she ran back and forth under the dense hedge. Limbs slapped my face and thorns tore the skin on my neck, back and arms. In despair, I looked toward the house. Mother was running across the pasture toward us. Lulabelle saw her too. Immediately, she turned and strolled to Mother.

Dad sold Lulabelle back to Sam the following day. Her gentleness must have been weakness from hunger. Or she had a Dr. Jeckel-Mr. Hyde personality.

"I should have known not to buy her when I saw those four white feet," said Dad.

"Why?" asked Linda.

"Because the saying goes: One white foot, buy him. Two white feet, try him. Three white feet, look well about him. Four white feet, go without him. And that skinny mare proved it."

Lulabelle's antics didn't dampen our love for horses. If a carnival came to town, we begged to ride the live ponies every round.

I spent many hours with my right hand extended in front of me holding imaginary reins. My left hand stroked an imaginary mane as my feet galloped over hills and jumped over streams in the timber behind our house. (That is, when I wasn't riding my cow.)

In the house, I was Linda's horse crawling from

room to room with her on my back and string reins in my mouth. She fed me popped corn for oats and bananas for ears of corn. We built a chair corral in the corner of the kitchen.

As time went by, we outgrew our pretending but we didn't outgrow wanting a real horse to ride. When Linda was twelve and I was four years older, we pooled our savings and bought Mabel, a black mare with NO white feet. She was a good horse for us girls. But she was a man-hater. If Dad tried to ride her, she bucked until he gave up. It wasn't just Dad; it was all men. We experimented and found this to be true.

During hay season, Linda climbed into the saddle on Mabel's back. She held a jug of cold water in one hand. Clutching the reins in her free hand, Linda rode Mabel to the hay field and gave the workers a drink. Rick wanted a lift back to the house. "Will your horse ride double, Linda?"

"Sure. Nancy and I ride double all the time. Climb on."

Rick climbed on behind Linda. Mabel bucked and bucked. Linda tried to calm her. Nothing helped. Rick fell off. Immediately Mabel stopped bucking. Linda rode her to back to the house. Rick walked.

Mabel looked out for Linda and me. One morning when Linda was bringing up the cows, the saddle slipped and Linda fell beneath the horse's body. Mabel stopped dead in her tracks and didn't move until Linda got up, tightened the saddle, then mounted her again. Together they drove the cows on to the barn.

One afternoon, we rode double on Mabel's broad bare back with Linda behind me. She began to tickle me under the arms. I lost my balance and fell beneath Mabel. At once, she stopped, turned her head, and stared at me lying on the ground. She didn't move until I was back topside and ready to go.

Mabel wasn't all good though. She had her bad days, too. I tightened the saddle girth around her middle then reached for the divided reins connected to her bit. One rein was pinned beneath Mabel's left front hoof.

I stood at her head and rubbed her muzzle. "Lift your foot, Mabel." She snorted and shook her head. I pulled at the rein. "Come on, move!" She didn't. Bending over from the waist, I pushed her leg with my shoulder. She lifted her foot. At the same time she bit the seat out of my slacks.

When cold, winter days drove us indoors, Linda and I found other games to play in our usual way. Indoor games started with fun and competition, led to angry arguments, and ended in a wrestling match between sisters.

Checkers were a challenge. If Linda saw she was loosing, she upset the card table. Checkers flew in all directions. "Ooops, sorry," she would say. I knew better. I grabbed her. The wrestling began; unless she got away. Then, the chase was on.

We played dominoes with much the same results as checkers.

Our favorite card game was Muggins. Many nights Mother and Dad joined us in the game. A dealer divided 150 cards equally among the players. We took turns building ten stacks of cards in sequence from one to fifteen. The first player to play all his cards was the winner. If someone didn't play when he could, one of us shouted "Muggins" and gave him a card. It wasn't a quiet game—at our house, nothing was quiet.

If rainy day boredom set in, Dad entertained us with a three feet long broom stick and five paper cups. The object was to balance the stick on end with the right hand, then let go of the stick, grab a cup from the floor and drop it over the top of the broom stick before it fell. The one with the most cups stacked on the stick won. The three of us tried until we stacked all five cups without a spill.

Or there was Dad's game played by holding the left ear lobe with the right hand and the right foot with the left hand. Across the room, he balanced a **Farm Journal** or **Successful Farming** magazine on end. First Linda, then I hopped to a magazine, bent down, and picked it up between our teeth without letting go of an ear lobe or the foot. With the magazine in our teeth, we hopped back to the starting line. The winner was the first one back holding lobe, leg, and literature in the proper places.

Dad gave us jobs to do. They rarely ended as intended. The metal glider and two metal lawn chairs needed a new coat of paint. Linda and I put on halter tops and short shorts. We each took a brush, a can of red paint and a chair. After the chairs were painted red, we complimented each other on our paint skills. Together, we started painting the glider.

My brush slipped. It painted a two inch strip down Linda's arm. "Oh, I'm so sorry," I said.

"Yeah. Sure you are," said Linda.

Five minutes later, Linda's brush fell. She painted my knee red.

Thus began the fencing of our paint-filled brushes. Linda covered me and I covered her with red paint from head to toe except for our eyelids. We ran out of paint.

Linda and I laughed at the sight. Dad chuckled. Mom frowned. She knew she had to supervise the gas wash of hair, body, and clothes. By the time the paint was off our bodies, Linda and I frowned, too.

If we painted with Dad, we moved as far from him as possible. He painted everything within ten feet of his brush. Dad didn't take time to wipe excess paint from his broom size brush. His paint policy was dip, drip, and drench. Before a job was done, he would be paint soaked to his shoulder and speckle-splattered all over. Mother made certain that Dad didn't paint any closer to the house than the white board fence fifty feet away. The inside jobs were left for her.

To be exact, I was three years and 363 days older than Linda unless it was a leap year. I was born October 24, 1942. Linda was born October 22, 1946. As the big sister, I pushed Linda around, ordered her about, and said, "Do it my way or I won't play."

As the little sister, Linda did things my way until she rebelled—at the age of five. From then on, we fought, wrestled, and chased. Such fun! Mother almost pulled her hair out hearing us "play." Dad laughed, wrestled, and egged us on, when he had a chance.

Sisters grow up. Situations may take them far away, but they remain special as only sisters may who play the games sisters play.

"Let's go to Grandpa and Grandma Lane's," said Dad. Linda and I dashed out the door and jumped in the car before he could blink an eye.

Going to Dad's parents' house was number one on our list for fun. They lived on a farm two miles east of us near Bruce. The best part of our visit was seeing which cousins were there to play with.

Dad's five sisters and four brothers had families of their own. Linda and I had twenty-one first cousins. One first cousin was married, and she had three young sons. Someone our age was always at Grandpa and Grandma Lane's when we went for a visit.

Day or night, when the weather was nice outside, Linda and I played Kick the Can or Hide and Seek with a dozen cousins.

Basically, I was a selfish child. Anytime I shared anything with my cousins they should have appreciated my generosity. But they didn't.

On December third, we gathered at Grandpa and Grandma Lane's house to celebrate Grandpa's sixty-fifth birthday. Twelve cousins were there. We played hard all evening. The red rash covering my body didn't slow me down. Earlier in the day, Mother had taken me to the doctor who had assured her that the rash was caused by an allergy; possibly

7
His, Hers & Theirs

caused by the laundry detergent she was using.

Two days later my rash had not disappeared. The good doctor re-diagnosed my rash. "She has the old-fashioned measles. Keep her in a dark room away from people. She's very contagious."

Two weeks to the day, Linda and our twelve cousins came down with the old-fashioned measles. Wasn't that generous of me? They didn't think so. Neither did their mothers and fathers.

Claude (Grandpa) and Mertle (Grandma) Lane's children were a combination of his, hers, and theirs. Grandpa's first wife died leaving him with two daughters ages four and one, plus a three-year-old son. He met and married Grandma. She had two sons ages twelve and fourteen. One year later, Dad became number one "theirs." Two years after Dad, a baby brother came along. Three years passed and grandma gave birth to her first daughter after four sons. The baby girl had two older sisters as well as five older brothers. Two years later another sister was born. Five years went by. Baby sister Nettie Lou was born. The family was complete.

Their three room farmhouse overflowed with family. Grandpa bought a three room farmhouse half a mile up the road. He moved everything; wife, kids, and house. Grandpa nailed the two houses together and pushed the people inside. Now they were a family of ten in a six room house.

Great Grandpa and Grandma Lane came to live with them. Hired hands slept in the boys' room. Dad slept three in a bed, three beds to a room.

Grandma cooked three big meals a day for the crowd. Benches lined either side of the long kitchen table. Dad recalled, "It was nothing unusual to have twenty people at the table for a meal."

Physically, Grandpa was tall with a bit of a belly in front. His glistening bald head was fringed with gray hair above both ears and at the nape of his neck. When he laughed, as he often did, Grandpa "tee, hee, heed" through clenched teeth.

Grandma was a square woman five feet tall. Her stoutness was accustomed to hard work! She could drive a team or shoe a horse as well as any man, better than many.

"Two of us boys were always getting in a fight," Dad told me. "Mom didn't interfere unless she thought we were getting too rough. Then she came at us swinging her broom." Dad went on. "One day, Mom piled six of us into the model T Ford. On our way to Bruce, the car slid off the muddy road into a ditch. Mom told us kids to stay in the car and watch the babies. She got out, lifted the car's back end, then the front end out of the ditch, and set it back on the road. She climbed in and drove us on to Bruce. That was my Mom."

Dad and his younger brother, Earl decided older brother Hugh was loafing too much. Hugh had suspended a chair by wires from the hayloft rafters. When he was supposed to be feeding the horses, Hugh climbed to the loft, settled into his swinging chair, and smoked a cigarette. One evening Dad and Earl cut the wires holding Hugh's chair almost in two. Then they hid in the hay and waited.

"Hugh climbed up into his chair," said Dad. "Earl and I watched him light up his cigarette. He leaned back. The wires snapped. Hugh fell into the hay below." Dad laughed. "I can still see the look on his face when he fell."

"He could have been hurt," said Linda.

"I know, but he wasn't," said Dad. "He was supposed to be helping us with the chores anyway."

"But you weren't doing chores," said Linda. "You were watching Uncle Hugh." Dad had to agree.

"Many a winter evening, Dad told us tales of home. "We had a black pony named Dan. Every kid for miles around loved Dan. One night there was a terrible electrical storm. The next morning, I went out and found Dan dead by the windmill. He had been struck by lightning. We held a regular funeral for Dan. Every one came to it and cried."

"Your Grandpa bought thirty head of wild Indian ponies south of Strasburg. They were thirty miles away. I was nine at the time. We all got on our horses, rounded up the ponies and drove them home. They were the wildest animals I'd ever seen. Dad shut them in the barn. They pushed down the door. He shoved a wagon in front of the open doorway. Then those ponies kicked out the side of the wooden barn. I don't know how he did it but Dad sold all the ponies and made money on the deal.

"Dad could make money on anything. Had to with all those mouths to feed."

"Bess and Nell were the best work horses he had. They'd pull a plow all day and never get winded. One night the barn caught fire and Bess and Nell were tied inside. We carried buckets of water but couldn't drown the flames. Dad tried running through the smoke and fire wrapped in a wet blanket. Nothing worked. Bess and Nell died in the fire."

"Nettie Lou wasn't more than six-years-old when she stood on the corral fence and called "Here,

Lulabelle. Come here, Lulabelle". Lulabelle came. That big sorrel work horse jumped the fence. Nettie Lous ran but Lulabelle trotted after her, edging closer and closer. Nettie darted through the back door and slammed the screen door behind her. Lulabelle stomped and pawed the back porch floor trying to get at little Nettie Lou."

"The depression in the thirties was shattering. Your Grandpa loaned milk cows to starving neighbors. His price was a calf a year from the cow until the neighbor could pay for the cow."

"Mr. Wheller owned the farm south of us," said Dad. "During the depression he didn't have enough money to pay his land taxes. Officials put his land up for sale for back taxes. Your Grandpa bought the farm, gave it back to Mr. Wheller and said, 'Pay me when you can.' He paid several years later, with interest."

Dad had a pet pig named Louie. The pig ran loose rooting up flowers and boys where ever he found them. "My mom didn't like Louie," Dad told us. "She was always chasing him with a stick."

"Where'd she chase him," I asked.

"Out of the garden, out of the house, out of the chicken pen, out of the yard, out of the flowers and out of the privy. Louie was a mischievous pig."

"No wonder Grandma didn't like your pig, Dad."

"You know what they say about pigs and the company they keep?" asked Dad.

"No, tell us."

"It goes like this. One night in late October, when I was far from sober, my feet began to stutter, so I lay down in the gutter, and a pig came near and lay down by my side. A lady passing by was heard to say, 'You can tell a man who boozes, by the company he chooses.' And the pig got up and slowly walked away."

On Easter Sunday the aunts, uncles and cousins went to Grandpa and Grandma Lane's house. Ham and all the trimmings were served buffet style since we had grown too big in numbers to fit around a table. After dinner, Grandpa went outside with all the grandkids to hunt for Easter eggs. "Hey, kids," shouted Grandpa. "Look here! Come and get the eggs the easter bunny left!" It puzzled me but I ran to see. I had just searched for jelly bean eggs where he stood. Yet, let Grandpa come up behind me and there'd be eggs on the ground all around.

Christmas Eve at Grandpa and Grandma Lane's was the highlight of the year as far as Linda and I and our cousins were concerned. All the clan came in for an oyster soup supper. Gifts were piled high under the Christmas tree. Before dinner, conversation was the same year after year. "I got your name. Who'd you get?"

"Not tellin'."

"Did you get my name?"

"Not tellin'."

"Did anybody get my name and buy me a present?"

"Not tellin'."

"Hey, everybody. I hear a knock on the front door."

There stood Santa Claus, red suit, white beard and all. "Ho, ho, ho! Merry Christmas boys and girls. Ho. Ho. Ho!" He passed out the gifts then left. Linda and I didn't wonder who was behind the beard. He was Santa. Why question it?

Then one Christmas Eve an older cousin shouted, "I know you, Santa. You're Uncle Dale." Sure enough. When Santa passed out gifts, Dad was no where in sight. After Santa left, Dad came back. That Christmas some grown-ups weren't too happy with one big-mouthed cousin.

Dad worked hard when he was growing up. At the age of nine, he shucked a load of corn before walking to school, if he went to school at all.

Attendance in the one room country school near his home depended on what had to be done at home or in the field first. By the time he was fifteen, Dad completed the eight grades at Baker's School and he began attending Sullivan High School. In his junior year, Dad dropped out. He was needed more at home than at school. The farm was big and the livestock were many.

While in school, Dad wrestled and boxed when he found the time. Dad was good in math but bad in English. And why not? A farmer had to have a head for figuring. But any horse understood plain English like "Haw" or "Git up" and "Whoa."

For Grandpa and Grandma Lane, his and hers grew to theirs and became ours. Through good times and glad times, through depression and death, Dad's family worked together, fought together, played together, and stayed together.

8
And Baby Makes 3

Mom's mother was Ethel. Her father was Frank Hogue. Mom was their first child and their last. After the baby made three, they added no more to the family tree.

Grandma Hogue was five feet seven inches tall and thin. She came from a family of nine children. Times were hard at her home. Grandma worked as a seamstress to help feed her brothers and sisters. If someone needed a new wardrobe, Grandma lived with them until all the sewing was done. Then she moved on to another job sewing while living in someone's home.

She was twenty-five (an old maid by standards in 1914) when she met and married Grandpa Hogue. He was four inches shorter and three years younger than Grandma. They moved into a tenant house two miles north of Windsor where, two years later, Mom was born.

Mom was ten-years-old when Grandpa bought his first farm across the road. They moved to their new home that went with the farmland. Grandpa and Grandma lived there until his death twenty-nine years later after forty-one years of marriage.

Mom grew up on the farm helping her mother with the chickens and the garden. Grandpa Hogue planted seed in the soil. He harvested the grain to sell or feed his horses, cattle, and hogs.

In 1930, Grandpa Hogue scooped a load of corn out of the crib and hauled it in town to the elevator for a sale. Mom recalled the day the Great Depression of the thirties began in her life. "Daddy came home from the elevator and said, 'Ethel, quit buying. Don't spend another cent. I just got ten cents a bushel for our corn. It would have brought a dollar a bushel yesterday. Times are going to get tough all over'."

Times did get tough all over. The fact that Mom's parents and Dad's parents held onto their land through the depression speaks in itself for their strong, industrious, thrifty farming tradition, and heritage.

How did my mom and dad meet? Dad said, "The Hog (ue) got out and she ran down the Lane." Mom didn't verify his tall tale.

Mom graduated from Windsor High School in 1935. The following year she went back to high school for post-graduate courses. Then she attended Sparks Business College and graduated in 1938.

In 1939, she met Dad for the first time through a mutual friend. He asked her for a date. She accepted. On their first date, Dad picked her up in his 1937 ford. "Where would you like to go, Wilma?" "It's up to you. I don't care." "Let's go to Sullivan," said Dad. "What do you want to do there?" "Why don't we park on the square and watch the people walk by?" said Mother.

And that's how they spent the evening. "Can I buy you something to eat or drink, Wilma?" asked Dad. "No, thank you. I'm just fine," said Mom. Her mother had told her never to spend a date's hard earned money.

Dale was hooked. He called Wilma Wednesday afternoon. "How about a date Saturday night?" "Sorry, I can't Saturday night," she told him. "Why not?" "I have a standing date with three girl-friends in Windsor on Saturday nights," said Mother. "Oh. Goodbye."

Dad didn't believe Mother had a date with girls. She had to be seeing another guy. Saturday night came. Dad drove to Windsor, parked the car at the curb, and watched people walk by. Fifteen minutes passed. Who did he see walking toward him? Petite Wilma. She was walking, laughing, and talking with three other girls. Dad called her over to his car. "How about a date tomorrow night?" "I'd like that," she said.

Eight months later they were married. "Why

45

didn't you go out with me that Saturday night, Wilma?" asked Dad.

"I'd just met you. I didn't know if you'd ask me for one date or two. I wasn't going to break my plans with old friends for a shot in the dark on Saturday night. Mother and Daddy always gave me a dime to have a good time with my friends."

On March 1, 1940 (Frank and Ethel Hogue's 26th wedding anniversary) Mom's uncle Bert married her—to Dad. Their wedding was small. Five people attended in all.

Mom and Dad moved into their first home one mile west of Dad's parents' place. The house had three rooms and no modern conveniences. Dad worked as a farmhand. He earned nine dollars a week. Not much, but two dollars bought a week's supply of groceries for the newlyweds. Mother raised turkeys for extra money. Their chickens laid eggs for the breakfast table. And after wedding present Jerse had her first calf, she gave milk twice a day.

On cold winter mornings, Mom finished her housework early then curled up under blankets to keep warm. She saved pennies on coal and wood for the stove. "I didn't drive the car anywhere alone," said Mother. "Gas cost too much. Once a week, I did go to my mother's and wash our clothes."

A year flew by. Grandpa Hogue bought a farm three miles west of Mom and Dad's tenant house. Dad agreed to farm the land. They moved to the five room house on the farm. One year later, I was born. And, once again, baby made three. Four years more and another baby made four.

"Nancy, you cried day and night from the time we brought you home from the hospital," said Mother. "Grandma Hogue was so proud of you she carried you everywhere and showed you off to everyone until you were sore all over."

The truth of the matter was I came into this world with my mouth open making much noise and haven't learned to shut up for over thirty years.

Mother recalled, "I wanted to watch over Nancy and protect her. But Dale said, 'Let her alone. She's got a big world to discover all by herself.' So I let her explore."

"As soon as she could walk she followed Spot, our fox terrier dog, everywhere. My stomach churned with fear every time I saw two-year-old Nancy disappear into the cornfield trailing after Spot," said Mother.

"Weren't you afraid she'd get lost?" asked Linda.

"I was scared to death until I found a solution. I

whistled for the dog. He came running out of the cornfield to me. Soon Nancy toddled out after him."

Mother shook her head. "I couldn't stand to watch Nancy with Dale when he fed the pigs."

"Why?" asked Linda.

"Nancy was two. She sat on the end gate of the feed wagon and watched the pigs fight for the ears of corn Dale threw out. When a pig ran close by, she jumped straddle its back and rode around the feed lot until it shook her off."

Once a week for as far back as I can remember, we went to Grandma and Grandpa Hogue's for Sunday dinner. Besides dinner, Sunday at Grandma and Grandpa Hogue's meant two new comic books, two new coloring books, or two new storybooks for two only grandchildren. Grandma and Grandpa were the spoilers. Linda and I were the spoilees.

One Sunday, we drove up to Grandma's house for dinner. Smoke billowed from the roof: not the chimney. Dad ran into the house. "Quick, Grandma. Get me a bucket. Your roof's on fire!"

"Oh, Dale. Quit your joking. You're such a tease," she laughed at him.

"It's no joke!" "Get me a bucket for water. Hurry!"

Mom ran in and shouted, "Mother, he's telling the truth. Your roof's burning!"

Grandma got the bucket. Dad carried water and climbed a ladder to the roof. He put out the fire in time. Little damage was done to the roof.

Afterwards, Mom said, "See what a tease you are, Dale. If I hadn't told Mother the roof was burning, she'd have stood in the kitchen and doubted your story while the house burned down around the both of you."

Grandma spent a year trying to improve Dad's manners at her dining room table every Sunday. Finally, she gave up and appreciated how much he enjoyed her delicious cooking. When we, her grandaughters, came alone, Grandma turned her good manners campaign on us. Grandma had a seventh grade education. She expected much more from Linda and me.

Wilma, their baby made three. Then Wilma married Dad. Eventually, there was me. After Linda came along, our family was complete. A relative is connected by blood; a friend by affection; and a neighbor by location. We're all connected by God. If we're not put on this earth to help each other, love one another, and laugh together, what are we here for?

9
Chicken Feed

To Linda and me, chicken feed meant new dresses. Mom made our dresses from flowered feed sacks. Mom, Linda, and I went with Dad to the feed store warehouse. We wandered up and down narrow aisles lined with towering fabric sacks of chicken feed. One sack displayed colorful yellow and pink flowers against a light green background. Another sack wore white tulips on a blue background. On and on stacked the warehouse's sack flower garden.

One day at the warehouse, Linda and I chose a sack with blue and red colors. Mom liked our choice. To the clerk, she said, "I'll need three sacks of chicken feed in the blue background with red rosebuds to make Nancy and Linda matching dresses." The clerk found two flowered sacks of feed right off. He couldn't locate a third sack of the same design.

"I must have three sacks or none," said Mother. "That's how much fabric it takes to make my daughters' dresses."

We joined in the search for sack number three. Each of us took an aisle and looked up one side and down the other. No luck. We were about to give up when, from two aisles away, the clerk shouted, "I found it!" The sack was squeezed in at the bottom of feed sacks stacked twelve high. Finally, we got the sack and carried out feed for chickens in fabric for children.

Mom bought feed for baby chicks in early spring. For her grown chickens, she ground corn through the feed grinder at the barn. During the summer months, Mom fed the chickens from her garden: radish tops, carrot tips, lettuce leaves, sweetcorn cobs, potato peels, and sand for the gizzard rounded out the grown chicken's daily diet.

Mother fried chicken, baked chicken, and fixed chicken with noodles. Her chickens didn't come dressed from the store ready to cook; Mom went to the chicken yard and caught fowls on foot.

Mom was the fastest chicken killer and feather plucker around. In her left hand, she carried a six feet long size number nine wire curved into a hook at the end farthest from her hand. She carried a bucket of boiling water in her right hand.

In the chicken lot, Mom sat the bucket of water on the ground. She strolled among the chickens with the hooked wire poised ready to strike.

A young rooster passed in front of her. Mom hooked his leg and drug him to her. With one hand, Mom gripped his feet. She laid his head on the ground, stepped on it, and pulled. Off came his head. Mom threw the rooster down and jumped back. The dismembered body flopped about splattering blood on the ground. Several minutes later, Mom again clutched the rooster's feet in her left hand. She dipped the dead chicken into boiling water. With great speed, she plucked feathers until that chicken was bare.

Anyone helping or watching her knew it wouldn't be long before there would be an aroma of chicken roasting in the oven or cut up chicken frying in the iron skillet on top of the kitchen stove.

Eggs filled a big space in our stomachs. Twice a day Mom gathered eggs from the nests in the old hen house.

Late one evening, Mom went alone to gather eggs. Three shelves of dark wooden boxes lined with straw stood along the hen house walls. Mother felt in the straw for eggs left by laying hens. She found two eggs in one nest, one egg in another, and two eggs in a third nest. At the next nest, Mom reached inside. Something in the dark nest felt rough, long, round—and cold. A snake! Mom jerked her hand back and ran to the house. "Dale, do something! I touched a snake in a nest at the hen house!" Dad picked up his old 12 gauge shotgun and loaded both barrels. Down at the hen house, Dad told her to point on the outside wall where the snake was lying inside. Mom pointed to a spot along the south side of the building. It's on the other side of that wall."

Dad squeezed the trigger. Boom! He squeezed the second trigger. Boom! He got that long egg-sucking black snake. Mom got more light in the hen house, too.

Sometimes Mom said to Linda and me, "Go gather the eggs." We went, but we didn't want to. Some hens laid their eggs in the nests then left; other hens stayed on the nest but merely clucked when we felt under them for their fresh eggs. Then there were those who wanted to keep their eggs. They pecked our hands.

Linda tried to get their attention while I edged my hand into the nest. That didn't work. My sneaking hand invariably was sighted and pecked. As likely as not, the old hen who put up a fight to protect her egg had no egg to protect. She had become unproductive and was only setting.

Mom sentenced an unproductive hen to jail for seven days. Jail was a three foot by four foot wire pen with a roof. It stood on four stilt poles beside the hen house. After one week, the hen was released. Once again, she became productive and contributed eggs. Why did jail cure a setting hen?

She needed the rest, I guess.

The eggs we didn't eat were culled, packed on cardboard in wooden crates, and sold to small owner-operated groceries in Sullivan.

For eight years after she and Dad were married, Mom raised and sold bronze turkeys. Linda and I could barely tolerate chickens, but we **were** bigger than any of them. Not so with turkeys. They were big—and unbearable. The only way we cared to see a turkey was dressed and ready to bake. Better still was a turkey roasted and ready to eat.

Turkeys were dumber than chickens. And chickens were lacking in common sense (or any sense for that matter). If caught in a rain, chickens eventually found shelter. Not turkeys. They stood in the rain and turned their nostriled beaks to the sky until they drowned. If turkeys survived their rain standing, they usually succumbed to pneumonia and died a week later.

When a rain came up, Linda and I had to help get those dumb turkeys inside. They didn't move forward or follow the leader. They circled and doubled back.

One afternoon the sky clouded over. Thunder rumbled for rain. I shooed turkeys toward shelter. A tom turkey turned. He fanned his tail into full

plume and ruffled up his feathers. Then he charged. A 35 pound, puffed up, fantailed turkey was big and looked even bigger when I was the five-year-old he aimed for. I dashed into the brooder house. The turkey darted after me—the door shut behind me just in time. Old tom turkey pranced his war dance and beat the door. I screamed and screamed until Mom came to my rescue.

When I was six and minus two front teeth, I raised six white ducks strictly for profit. They grew fat for market. The poultry man stopped at our house to buy fryers from Mom. I walked up to him and said, "Will you buy by sith ducks?"

"Sick ducks? I can't buy sick ducks," said the poultry man.

"Not sick. SITH."

"Let me see—I'll make an exception for a nice little girl like you without any teeth. I'll take those sick ducks off your hands for 75 cents a piece."

"THEY'RE NOT SICK! They're one, two, three, four, five, sith ducks."

"It's a deal then" said the poultryman. "I'll do you a favor and buy your six sick ducks."

He paid me $4.50 and left with the ducks. I wondered about him. Anyone could tell those ducks

51

were fine and fat, not sick. Besides, what kind of poultryman was he if he really thought he was buying sick ducks from me?

Linda and I rocked chickens to sleep when we could find nothing better to do. Linda grabbed a chicken, tucked his head under a wing and rocked him back and forth in her arms. In no time, the chicken was asleep and stayed that way from five to fifteen minutes.

I was ten when I first raised chickens for my 4-H project. Fifty Austria White chickens were supposed to be my full responsibility. But if Mom hadn't stepped in to feed and water them most of the time, my projects would have died. All fifty of them.

For three years I washed up three dirty white chickens for 4-H county fair day in July. It was a trying task to wash feathers and feet while dodging pecking beaks. How the two hens and one rooster hated their baths. Me, too.

My chickens always won first place at the county fair. Why? Because not another 4-Her in Moultrie County raised Austria Whites.

To me, fowls are foul. Foul in smell; foul in soil; foul in favor; and foul in toil. Fowls treated Linda and me foul—not fair. But we were the first to eat if fried chicken and roast turkey were there. Chicken feed? You bet! Find the fabric and fatten the fowl. Soon it'll be time for new dresses and nice dinners.

Recess. The short intermissions between readin', ritin', and 'rithmetic. "Linda, what have you learned at school?" asked Grandpa Hogue.

"How to jump rope."

"Let me put it another way. What are your favorite subjects?"

"Recess, recess, and recess."

Bruce School stood on a hill facing west, south of Bruce. There were two rooms: grades one, two, and three learned in the north room; grades four, five, and six sat in the south room. Modern desks filled both rooms. Desk lids raised for book storage, attached swivel chairs made it easier to get in and out of the desks, and both rooms had desks in all sizes for big or little student.

Linda was extra tiny and wirey. I was the exact opposite: chubby and growing fast for my age. As adults, Linda and I both ended up five feet tall. I stopped growing when I was twelve she grew until she was sixteen.

Linda's first grade teacher gave her the smallest seat in school but her feet still didn't touch the floor. When Dad heard about it, he said, "My girl can't sit in school all day dangling her feet—that's too uncomfortable."

He hauled blocks of wood to school. Under

10
The 3Rs: Recess, Recess, Recess,

Linda's desk Dad placed two wood blocks two inches thick. Linda sat down. Still, her feet didn't touch: they dangled in midair. Dad nailed two more two inch thick blocks of wood on top of the others. Linda sat down. She rested her feet on the wood blocks. Perfect fit.

When school started for Linda's second year, Dad removed the top two inch blocks of wood. When Linda was a third grader the next year, Dad removed the remaining two blocks of wood. At last, Linda sat in her tiny desk and rested her feet on the floor.

Linda and I enjoyed school. Most of the time we worked hard to earn good grades, but during the second grade, Linda hit a snag in spelling and science. Report cards came out and her grades were lower than expected. For the next six weeks, she struggled to improve.

When report cards came out again, her grades were higher but still lower than mine. "Linda, what a good report card," said Mother and Dad. "You came up in spelling and science. Keep working. We're so proud of you."

Linda ran outside to play. I handed my report card to Mother and Dad then waited for praise. They studied my grades. "You did the same as last time."

I waited. Was that all they were going to say? Finally, I spoke up. "My grades are lots better than Linda's. You didn't say you were proud of me, but you're proud of her."

"We're proud of you, too, Nancy," said Dad. "But, you see, we're trying to build up Linda's confidence. We're afraid she's going to be a midget."

A midget? My sister a midget? Jealousy diminished for a while. How could I be jealous of my sister, the midget?

Then she started to grow and so did sibling jealousy.

Every school day the yellow bus picked Linda and me up at 7:45 A.M. We rode fifteen miles on country roads to get to Bruce school three miles away, with a bus load at 8:30.

There were five students in my first grade class. In the second grade our number grew to six. Barbara was the new girl's name. I liked Barbara. In fact, I idolized Barbara. She was pretty. Her long, black hair hung in curls down her back. My hair was short, straight, and dishwater blonde. It hung in strings. Mom said a "cowlick" made my bangs stand straight up in the middle of my forehead. But I didn't remember being licked by a cow on my forehead. Lots of other places, but not there.

Barbara came to school one morning with a baby tooth missing. Her tooth next to the right front tooth had fallen out during the night while she slept. The black space in her mouth was beautiful. After school, I jumped off the bus and cornered Dad. Pointing at the tooth next to my right front tooth, I said, "Pull it!"

"It isn't loose enough," said Dad.

"I want it pulled now. Barbara has hers out. I want mine out, too."

Throughout the evening, Dad's stout fingers rocked, twisted, and bent my tooth against the gum. He tied one end of a string around my tooth, the other end to a doorknob, then slammed the door. The string broke—my tooth stayed in. Dad went back to prying with his fingers. By and by, just before bedtime, the tooth came out. Dad sat back and shook his head. He examined his aching index finger and thumb. I could hardly wait until morning. I'd go to school and show Barbara my new space just like hers.

Barbara and I didn't see each other during summer vacation. When school began in the fall the number of third graders was back to five. Barbara

had moved away and I never heard from her again.

To be the first one done, I rushed through arithmetic assignments skipping three or four problems every day. I darted up the aisle and laid my paper on Mrs. Homer's desk. After two weeks of problem skipping, she kept me in during last

recess. "Nancy, you didn't do three out of twelve problems again today."

"I didn't?"

"I've warned you and warned you. This carelessness must stop. Slow down. Do all the problems. Check to be sure before you hand in any more papers. Understand?" I nodded. "If you hand in another unfinished assignment, I'll spank you."

Tears filled my eyes. Mrs. Homer meant it. I had seen her spank other students with the long paddle hanging over the cloak room door. It wasn't for me. From then on, I wasn't the first one to hand in my arithmetic assignment because I checked and double checked for unfinished problems.

LeRoy, Brenda, Eugene, Kay, and I started first grade together at Bruce. For six years, we stayed together. I don't recall studying regular subjects. I do remember knitting string dishrags, weaving scarves on handmade looms, drawing dinosaurs with bulletin board committees, and making paper mache' alligators. But, there must have been lessons sometime during school. Where else would I have learned how to read and write?

A barrel-shaped coal stove stood eight feet tall near the school's inner wall at Bruce. Every summer the stove was covered with a new coat of silver paint. In winter, our room's strongest boy carried cobs and coal from a shed south of the school building. He came early and built a fire then kept it going all day. Mrs. Dokan, the other teacher, paid him seventy-five cents a week for his work.

At the beginning of each school year, Mrs. Dokan chose two girls to clean blackboards, pound erasers, and dust mop floors every day during last recess. On Friday's noon hour, we washed blackboards and wiped furniture. For this, we were paid seventy-five cents apiece. The way I looked at it, being school janitor was a paying privilege.

We didn't have to clean the bathrooms in the school. There weren't any. Two white outhouses occupied opposite back corners of the school yard; girls to the left, boys to the right. The colder the weather, the faster the students' toilet break.

Cold drinking water was available at the rusty pump in front of the school. Each student brought his own initialed tin cup to drink at the pump. When not in use, the cups sat on a shelf above the dinner bucket shelf in the cloak room.

Our school playground was shaded by eleven age-bent trees. At recess time, we ran off pent-up energy and yelled away frustrations playing Red Rover, Dodge ball, Run for Your Supper, Bear on the Mountain, and chase, chase, chase in the dirt.

Softball games highlighted springtime. Allenville's country school team was the rival for us to beat. Their school had eight grades; therefore, their players were bigger and older than ours. A player's sex made no difference so long as he or she played good ball. Equality was practiced in our athletic department long before we knew it had a name.

Mom and Dad attended our school's programs for parents. On stage, I looked at the audience and spotted Dad immediately. Who could miss him? His shiny bald head stood out because he sat straight and tall then stretched his neck. Dad's face peered over everyone's head. After finding Dad in the audience, neither Linda nor I looked his way again. One day, after our school play, Dad said, "Nancy and Linda, why don't you look at me when you're on stage?"

"You know why, Daddy," said Linda. "If we look at you, you make funny faces. Then we forget our lines and giggle."

Linda and I rode the school bus two hours a day both ways. We were the first ones on and the last ones off. It was a long, noisy, and bumpy ride. Every stop to let students off meant "fruit basket upset" or time to change seats.

I began first grade in the autumn of 1948. If there had been a country school kindergarten or I had been one year older, I wouldn't have ridden a bus to school. I would have walked to Harmony School down the road from our home. Harmony, a one room school house for eight grades stood at a T road one-fourth mile west of us. One teacher taught all eight grades. I often ran to the school yard at recess time when I was four and Mrs. Deitz, the teacher, would invite me to school for the rest of the afternoon.

During the summer of 1948, Harmony School was closed. The building was sold and moved away to be re-opened as a home. All that remained at the T road was the school yard pump.

Before Harmony school closed, Mom, Dad, Linda, and I went to its Christmas party every year. I screamed, clung to Mother, and refused to sit on Santa's knee. Linda did, too. We didn't know the knee came from home. With his broad shoulders and husky built, Dad ho-ho-hoed behind a white beard and red suit at home, in schools, and at church during the yuletide season. We didn't know it was Dad. Santa did know a lot about Linda and me. But he was supposed to. Didn't Santa watch children all year long?

Years later, Dad chuckled as he said to Linda and me, "You girls were the funniest things. When I perched you both on my knee you cried the loudest of anyone there. Imagine that, afraid of your own dad!"

Linda and I wore T-shirts and jeans to school. We changed T-shirts every other day and jeans twice a week. Mom's Monday wash would have otherwise been too large to do in one day—if we'd had enough clothes to change into more often.

Town school was quite a change for me, the seventh grade country girl: from a total enrollment of thirty-five to four hundred students, from tin cups at the pump to indoor fountains, from white out-houses to indoor restrooms and P.E. showers, from coat room hooks to lockers with combinations, from one teacher for three years to six teachers for one day, from T-shirts and jeans to dresses, and from a class of five to a class of one hundred twenty five.

At Bruce school, I knew everyone by name; they were my friends. At junior high school, no one was my friend. Loneliness and shyness became my constant companions. For six weeks, I made no close friends.

One day during noon hour play, I sat on the school steps all alone. Tears spilled down my cheeks and spotted my dress front. A teacher passed by, saw my tears, found the trouble, and introduced me to four girls my age. "This is Nancy. She'd like to play with you girls," said Miss Storm.

That's all I needed. In no time, we were friends. Later, my girl friends said, "Dianne knew you and made you sound yucky. She said you rode a cow. Do you?" I told them about Princess. "It sounds different hearing you tell about your cow," said my friends.

When spring came, I gave a slumber party. Girls jumped out of the car and dashed for the barn. Altogether they shouted, "I want to be first to ride Nancy's cow!"

"Learning never ends," Dad told Linda and me. "Don't ever close your minds. Keep them open, ready to accept or reject new ideas after careful consideration. Look at me. I've used my brain so much that it wore off all the hair on top of my head."

Strange how much you've got to know,
Before you know how little you know.

Anonymous

58

Linda was five and I was nine when Mom spent two weeks in the hospital. Dad cooked makeshift meals for the three of us. One evening, he said, "I'll fix gravy tonight, girls. YOUR MOM TOLD ME HOW TODAY. Nothing to it."

Dad poured bacon grease into a big iron skillet on the stove.

"Mom doesn't use that much grease," said Linda.

"Who's doing this? You or me?"

"You, Daddy."

"Let's see. Your mom said to add a handful of flour." Dad put his hand into the cannister and pulled out a fistful of flour. He dropped the flour into the sizzling bacon grease. Dad stirred. He added milk and stirred again. He added more milk and stirred faster. Gravy ran over the side of the skillet. Dad picked up the skillet and dashed outside. He poured thick gravy into the dogs' dishes.

Back at the stove, Dad added milk and stirred. The gravy was still too thick. It overflowed onto the burner. Dad darted back outside with the skillet in his hand dripping gravy all the way. He filled the cats' feed bowls with thick gravy.

Again, Dad returned to the stove. This time he added two glasses of water and stirred. At last, he

11 Please Pass The Gravy

sighed, "Okay, girls. Sit down. Supper's ready."

"Daddy, why did you make so much gravy?" asked Linda.

"Never mind."

"Dad," I said. "If you hadn't used so much flour and grease and wouldn't have—." "I know," interrupted Dad. "My handful's bigger than your mom's. Eat before the gravy gets cold."

After supper, we had gravy left in our bowl. The two dogs left gravy in their bowls and the twenty-two cats left gravy in their bowls. When Dad made gravy, he made **lots** of it for everybody!

On a brisk October morning, Mom got us up before five. "Hurry, girls. We're going to Grandpa Hogue's and butcher hogs today." We arrived at Grandpa's house before sunrise. Fire blazed under a big black kettle set near a tree in the feed lot.

Linda and I went to the house with Mom. Grandpa and Dad went to the barn. Soon we heard a shot, then another. Two hogs were dead. We knew Dad had shot them in the head. "Come out and watch, girls," yelled Dad from the feed lot.

Linda and I then raced out the door and joined them in the feed lot.

"Help me hook the hind legs to the pulley ropes in the tree, Frank," said Dad to Grandpa. With that task finished, Dad hoisted the carcasses up to hang upside down in the tree. "Now for the scalding barrels," said Dad. He positioned two big barrels beneath each carcass. "Okay, Wilma. Bring on the hot water," said Dad.

Mom and Grandma filled both barrels with boiling water. Dad untied the pulley rope and lowered one hog into the scalding water. Then he did the same with the other hog. Three minutes later, Dad hoisted the carcasses out of the water and back into the tree. All the hair was scalded off the two pigskins.

Dad sharpened his long bladed butchering knife while the blood and water drained from the hogs for fifteen minutes. Cutting began. Dad gutted the carcasses. He then sliced off slabs of fat and tossed them into the big black kettle swinging from an iron pole tripod above the fire. Fat melted and sizzled in the kettle. Dad threw in cracklin's from the carcass. He threw in the catfish or tenderloin. Everyone lingered around the kettle. Grandma pulled the meat out of the fat, sliced it, then passed around the delicious pork tenderloin for us to eat with our fingers.

Meanwhile Dad finished cutting up both carcasses. "Time to cure the sausage," said Grandpa.

Linda and I went to the basement with him. He pressed meat through the sausage grinder. Grandma joined us in the basement. She mixed sage, salt, and pepper into the sausage with both hands. She then stuffed the seasoned sausage into pig gut skins and hung them in the smokehouse. In the kitchen, Mom sugar-cured the hams with a brown sugar mixture. Linda and I would sneak brown sugar to eat when no one was looking.

Dad soaked bacon slabs in salt brine. He then hung the bacon and hams in the smoke house with the sausages.

Next would be the lard. Dad carried the lard press outside to the big iron kettle in the feed lot. The fire had been extinguished earlier. The kettle was cool to the touch, and the fat inside the kettle was solid. Mom ladled fat from the kettle into the press. Dad pushed lard through the press separating out cracklin's and sediment. In metal five gallon cans, Mom sealed lard for frying and baking.

Grandma slit the two hogs' heads then boiled them. Later, she made mincemeat pie from the boiled-out brains and marrow.

On a cold morning in December, Dad shot a cow, skinned and gutted her, then wrapped the carcass in a sheet and hung it by its hind legs in the barn. So long as the weather stayed freezing cold, Dad cut portions of beef from the carcass for Mom to grind or fry when she needed it. If the radio reported a warming trend on the way, Dad let down the beef carcass, brought it into the kitchen and handed it over to Mom. She canned the remaining meat by cutting up raw beef, filling quart jars with it, then cold-packing the beef in a giant canner on top of the kitchen stove.

We drank sassafras tea in the winter. Dad dug up the dirty roots of a sassafras tree, handed them to Mom and said, "Fix us all some sassafras tea. We need it to thin our blood for better health."

In early spring, the wild blackberry briars bloomed. Dad fashioned pails for blackberry picking by connecting wire handles to lard cans. Armed with pails, Linda and I went with Mom to the woods. We filled our pails with juicy blackberries and pricked our bodies with jagged briars. Chigger bugs hid among the briars. They itched their way under our skins.

When winter drew near, we went back to the woods with our buckets, and gathered walnuts under the walnut trees, as well as hickory nuts under the hickory trees. Dad spread the walnuts out in the driveway. Trucks and cars drove over them for two weeks. They squeezed out the staining juices and stripped off the outer skins of the walnuts. Once more, Linda and I put the walnuts (now dried) into a bucket. We cracked the shells and picked out nutmeats for Mom's baking and candy making.

Summertime meant cherry picking, peach picking, and apple gathering time. We had the peach trees in our garden to share. Our neighbors shared their cherry and apple trees with us.

Mom's vegetables grew south of the house. In early spring, Linda and I planted radishes with Dad's homemade seed shaker (a jar with tiny holes punched in the lid). We planted row after row of onion sets and watered Mom's tomatoes, cabbage, and pepper plants. Rows of carrots, beets, green beans, lettuce, peas, corn, and potatoes also grew in Mom's garden.

Dad helped raise the sweet corn. He grew bumper crops of golden banner sweet corn. Linda and I sold the surplus ears of sweet corn to customers in town.

One day when I was ten, Linda, Dad, and I loaded ears of sweet corn into the back of our old truck and went to town. I marched up to a door and knocked. A strange woman came to the door. All at once, I was nervous and tongue tied. "D-d-d-do you want to buy andy p-p-popcorn?" I asked.

"Popcorn? No, I can't eat popcorn."

Dad sat in the truck and laughed. "We don't have any popcorn to sell," he yelled. "But we do have good sweet corn."

The woman liked sweet corn. She bought two dozen ears. A reliable saleslady I was not. But Dad had a good laugh every time he told how I tried to sell popcorn instead of sweet corn.

By the time the first snow fell, Mom and Dad had filled our dirt floor cellar with canned green beans and corn, pickled red beets in quart jars, and lime pickles in brine. From the ceiling rafters, Dad hung bunches of garden onions. They dried until Mom needed them in the kitchen. Dad buried garden carrots, potatoes and turnips in sand to keep for winter time eating.

Oleo for cooking came from the store white and sealed in a cellophane bag. Linda and I took turns squeezing the yellow in.

For pucker power, we ate raw rhubarb from the garden and almost-ripe persimmons from the tree in the front yard.

Mom fried most of our food in bacon grease:

eggs, potatoes, steaks, green tomatoes, pork chops, fish, and mushrooms.

On Sunday evening, Dad fried hamburgers smothered in cheese and onions. After supper, he popped corn for nightime muching.

Dad loved to eat. Any good time revolved around food, food, food. He invited friends over for hand-cranked ice cream made with cream fresh from the cow and eggs fresh from the chickens. In town, Dad treated Mom, Linda and me at the Root Beer Stand or Frigid Creme regularly. We stopped at the first food place we came to.

Dad's eating habits were unique. He salted bananas before he ate them. He covered gravy with mustard and black pepper before he took a bite. Dad's favorite bedtime snack was a glass of warm milk stuffed with crumbled crackers.

In season, Dad cut fresh sweet corn off the cob. He added cut up tomatoes, butter, salt, pepper, and chopped onions; stirred the mixture together; then topped it all with hot gravy. What a tasty treat for him—and a messy sight for me to see. Mother's favorite treat was fresh red or white radishes dipped in salt and eaten with bread and butter. To me, mayonnaise sandwiches, mustard sandwiches, or peanut butter and lettuce sandwiches were good eating. That was way back then, not now. Linda loved chocolate covered malt balls. She pronounced them "moth balls." Heads turned her way with sickening stares when she said, "Daddy, buy me some moth balls to eat."

Dad was tough everywhere but in his stomach. Linda and I had to be careful what we said at the table. Dad insisted that the conversation be light and pleasant. If Linda or I said anything about a sick cow or finding a dead skunk, Dad lost his dinner.

Whether good or bad, we followed our own eating habits. "You don't feel well? Eat something. It'll make you feel better."

"You did a good job. Let's have something to eat."

"Clean your plate. Be a good girl. You want seconds? Great."

Dad had his unusual favorites in foods but he didn't like to try any new recipes. From my 4-H cooking project book, I fixed cheese fondue sandwiches for Dad. The recipe called for cheese sandwiches placed in a baking dish then covered with tomatoe sauce and baked for fifteen minutes. I placed my just-finished fondue in front of Dad. "What's that?" he asked.

"A new recipe. Try it." I said.

"Do I have to?"

"Please, Daddy."

He took one bite. As he left the table, he said to me, "Nancy, leave it to you to try something new. Are you sure that's for eating?"

Dad's definitely a meat, potatoes and gravy man. But I couldn't eat that recipe, and the dogs or cats wouldn't touch it either.

Planting, picking, gathering, butchering, canning, and planning for food filled many a day. To some, it may have sounded like work, but not to us. We were self-sustaining. We didn't pay a middleman. Our food went straight from us, the producer, to us, the consumer. And we loved to eat.

64

12
Doctor Dad

Dad diagnosed home remedies for our medical problems. With us and animals, Doctor Dad consulted a doctor or a vet as the last resort.

"Dad, I've got a stomach ache," said Linda.

"I'll mix up some salt and soda in warm water for you to drink," said Dad. "It'll either settle your stomach or make you throw up." He was correct. If you took salt and soda in water, you did one or the other.

"I've got a headache."

"Take some syrup pepsin."

"I've got a belly ache."

"Take some syrup pepsin."

"I cut myself on the barbed wire fence."

"Get out the "man or beast" salve."

If Linda, Mom, or I cut a foot or hand, Dad brought out his "man or beast" salve, gauze, and tape. He washed, treated, and bandaged our injuries until we were healed. We had great faith in our Doctor Dad.

Dad didn't limit his doctoring to humans, he cared for the animals, too. If our cow, dog, or cat's skin was cut, Dad doctored it with the same remedy of "man or beast" salve, gauze, and tape he used for us.

One time that Dad didn't do the doctoring was

when I was five and was burned while helping Mother fry a pork steak. She dropped a heaping spoonful of lard into the iron skillet on the burner. Soon the grease began to sizzle in the skillet. Mother dipped the steak in flour. "Let me put the steak in the skillet to cook, please," I begged. Mother relented and consented. I stood on my toes in front of the skillet and barely saw over the side of it. First, I laid the back side of the steak in bubbling grease. Then, for some unknown reason, I dropped the rest of the steak into the skillet. Hot grease splattered my face. Dad grabbed the nearest clean cloth; one of baby Linda's diapers. He covered my "fried" face and diagnosed a doctor. Scooping me up in his arms, Dad dashed to the car. He laid me in the back seat and said, "Lie still. Don't move the diaper."

With lightning speed, Dad drove us to town blasting the car horn all the way. Second degree burns covered my face. I was lucky. To Dad, Dr. Lawsman said, "Good thing you covered her face with a diaper. Air exposure would've caused third degree burns. And that would've meant skin grafting. As it looks now, I don't think she'll have any scars when the burns heal."

For six weeks, wherever I went everyone stared at me—the little girl whose face was black with ugly scabs. We went to Grandpa Lane's house. Cousin Anita hid her head under a sofa cushion. She wouldn't look at me. She refused to play. "Nancy's too scary. Like a monster," she cried.

At night, my eyes swelled shut. Every morning, Dad spread cream from a tube on my eyelids then forced them open.

Mom, Dad, Linda and I went to a restaurant for lunch. A waitress came to our table. She saw my scabs. "What's wrong with her face?" Dad motioned for her to come closer. He leaned toward her and whispered, "Smallpox."

She fled. No one would wait on us. Finally, we got up and left. Dad laughed all the way to the restaurant across the street. "It was worth not being served," he chuckled. "Did you see her face, Wilma?"

"Yes, I saw her face," Mother replied. "But I didn't see the humor. Don't say smallpox at this restaurant, Dale. I'm hungry."

On a Sunday morning when Linda was three, her forehead fought with a cultivator sweep and lost.

Mother called Doctor Swain (Doctor Lawsman's replacement). He met us at his office. Doctor Swain sewed together the gash in Linda's forehead with three neat stitches. Instead of a girl with a curl in the middle of her forehead, Linda became the kid with a skid in the middle of her forehead.

On a Sunday afternoon when I was seven, we were all at Grandpa and Grandma Hogue's house, as usual. Material, pins, and needles cluttered the living room floor. Grandma sat in the middle of it showing Linda and me how to make doll clothes. I crawled across the floor. "Ouch!", I cried. Pain shot through my right knee. Something stabbed into it. I sat back and straightened out my leg.

"Wait. Don't move your leg," said Dad. "A needle's sticking in your knee." He pulled out the needle and examined it. "Call the doctor, Wilma. Half of this needle's missing."

Again Dr. Swain met us at his office. He bound my leg to a wooden splint. The next morning, x-rays were taken and developed. Dad studied the inside view of my knee with Doctor Swain.

"There's the rest of the needle," said Doctor Swain as he pointed to a black line on the X-ray. "We'll have to hospitalize her and operate."

"Wait a minute," said Dad. "Will her knee be stiff after surgery?"

"There's a chance it will."

"Her knee doesn't hurt now. I say wait," said Dad. "If it starts bothering her, **then** we operate."

Reluctantly, Dr. Swain agreed. They didn't operate. That was twenty-five years ago. To this day, the needle hasn't given me any trouble.

Mom and Dad stressed that sickness or pain need not be dwelled on. Respecting injuries and ills was wise but letting them dominate the day was foolish for all concerned.

Dad was strong and thus carried heavy loads. When he was twenty-nine-years-old, he had hoisted two one-hundred pound sacks of chicken feed onto his broad shoulders. On the way to the chicken house, he slipped on a patch of ice, fell, and damaged a disc in his lower back pinching his sciatic nerve. Dad didn't slow down; he didn't know how. Therefore, his injury didn't completely heal. The disc continued to slip in and out of place and eventually it deteriorated from the wear and tear. A spinal specialist prescribed a brace to immobolize his back.

Leather-cushioned steel bands circled Dad's body six inches above and six inches below his waist. Rubber sections with buckles and a zipper held the bands firmly in place. His back remained immobile. He lived with the discomfort of the brace and the pain of his back. But they didn't get him down: He had work to do. Dad's back brace was his constant companion.

I brought home all common household communicable diseases and shared them with Linda. I gave her measles, mumps, whooping cough, and chicken pox.

Polio epidemics raged throughout the nation in the early 1950's. Mom and Dad insisted that Linda and I rest every afternoon during long, hot summer days. "Don't get too tired, girls," said Dad. "Is your throat sore? Do you have a stiff neck?"

We didn't go swimming: "You might be exposed to polio." We didn't go shopping in big cities: "You might be exposed to polio." We didn't go to county fairs: "You might be exposed to polio."

Mom and Dad went to the State Fair in August. They left us at Grandma and Grandpa Hogue's: "We don't want you girls in a crowd. You might get polio."

Grandpa and Grandma Lane moved from their home on the farm to a house in town. One afternoon we visited them and played with our new friends, the Theoburg children, across the street.

The next afternoon the telephone rang at home. When Mother hung up, she closed her eyes and took a deep breath.

"What's wrong, Wilma?" asked Dad.

"Remember the Theoburg children Nancy and Linda played with all afternoon yesterday?" Dad nodded. "That was your mom on the phone. Both children came down with polio of the throat this morning. They're in the hospital. No one knows how bad they are yet."

We went about doing normal chores and play with one noticeable difference. Mom asked us more often, "do you have a stiff neck. Does your throat hurt? Do your legs hurt?"

We didn't. It didn't. And they didn't. I'm happy to say that the Theoburg children were home in three weeks and we played together again. A scar in the hollow of their throats was the only sign that they had had polio.

On a hot summer day in the polio epidemic years, Linda became violently ill and her temperature shot up to 104 degrees. Her throat grew so sore she couldn't swallow. Nothing stayed in her stomach. Doctor Swain came. His first concern was lowering her burning fever.

No one mentioned polio. Everyone thought it. For two days and nights, my nine-year-old mind knew Linda was getting polio. All thoughts of teasing her vanished. When she was awake, I stayed beside

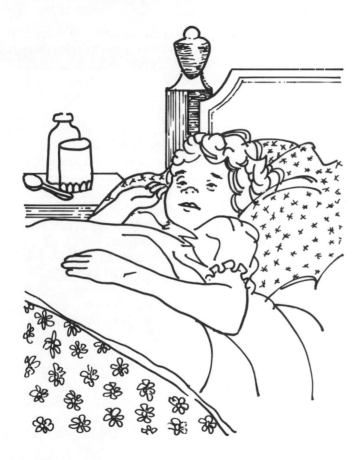

her bed; reading to her, singing to her, holding her hand—whatever she wanted.

Linda fought fever, nausea, and throat pain. At length, Doctor Swain diagnosed her illness as severely infected tonsils. They would have to come out. (But not in the summer with polio striking all around us.) Penicillin brought Linda's infection under control. She soon felt as good and as mischievous as before.

In 1955, Salk's anti-polio vaccine became available to the public. We lined up for our shot. The devastating polio scare was a thing of the past—if people vaccinated themselves and their children against the crippling (and sometimes deadly) virus.

Dad didn't take me to the doctor when I pushed a soybean up my nose. He worked and worked until he squeezed it out. "Don't do that again, Nancy," said Dad. "Why did you do it in the first place?"

I shrugged. "Wanted to see how it felt, I guess."

I was twelve when I decided to be a veterinarian. It began when I first helped Dad deliver a calf. The birth was uncomplicated but the newborn calf wasn't breathing.

"Hit the calf in the ribs, Nancy," said Dad. "I can't leave the cow." I pounded my fist against the calf's ribs behind his front shoulders. He let out a

69

feeble 'baah' then started breathing normally.

After that night I helped Dad deliver many, many calves. No two births were the same; no two calves were alike.

A heifer's first calf was too big to be born. The ordeal began one day in May when Dad and I found Frances under a walnut tree in the timber behind our house. She was dying. The calf was half born and was dead. Frances was paralyzed in her hind quarters. Her tongue hung out of her mouth. Each labored breath sounded as if it were her last.

"Get the vet," ordered Dad.

I ran. My bare feet pounded against the hoof-worn path. Five minutes later, I stopped and looked around. I was in dense timber. I should have been to the barn by now. In my excitement, I had run west instead of east toward the house and the telephone. I turned around and ran back along the path. Five minutes later, Dad called from the top of the hill, "What are you doing, Nancy?"

"I ran the wrong way!" I yelled back. But I didn't slow down—I dashed on to the house. When Dad ordered, I obeyed.

The vet came. Frances, the cow survived. "You should kill her," the vet told Dad. "She'll never walk again."

Dad didn't kill her. The next day we rolled her down the hill to a grassy bed under the cottonwood tree near a brook. She couldn't move; not even for a drink from the brook. Once a day, everyday, we walked a rough half-mile trip back to Frances. Dad carried water for her thirst; I carried corn for her strength; and Linda carried oats for her energy. In June, we rolled her over each day. In July, she rolled herself over and swatted flies. One hot August evening, we stepped into the clearing. Frances was **standing**. In September, Dad pulled, I pushed, and Linda tugged Frances up and down the winding path to the barn. October came and went. Frances walked with a slight stagger.

In November, Dad loaded Frances into the truck and took her to the sale barn. She brought $75.00. Not a bad price for a cow then; but not a good price for 900 hours of labor. We earned about eight cents an hour for caring for her. But our compassion was free and sincere. No other cow received more humane, devoted care. No on complained about the work since Frances needed us. She knew it. And we knew it.

A two-day-old calf was failing fast. "I don't know what to make of him," Dad said. "He doesn't suck. Acts like he doesn't know how. Fix him an egg nog, girls. We'll try to save him.''

At the house, Linda and I beat together raw eggs and warm milk. Then we poured the mixture into an empty Pepsi bottle. Linda carried it to the barn. I knelt beside the ailing calf and lifted his limp head to open his mouth. Linda poured egg nog down his throat. I closed his mouth and held it shut. Linda stroked his throat until he swallowed. We fed the sick calf one slow swallow after another until the bottle was empty. For the next two days, Linda and I repeated the slow egg nog feeding three times a day.

The calf survived. After much coaxing, he learned how to suck milk from his mother. He did silly things; he ran into barn walls, fences, and other cattle. We named him Silly.

As Silly grew, he preferred people to his own kind. He regularly broke down the pasture fence and laid at our feet like a dog in the front yard. Finally, he became such a nuisance that Dad had to sell Silly.

Domesticated animals need their masters for food, shelter, and love. They know it. Their masters know it. In return, some animals give milk or the wool off their backs. Others obey every signal of command and are eager to do so.

As long as Doctor Dad was around to diagnose and fulfill their needs, animals and people felt secure at our house.

13
Learning The Value Of Learning

Dad taught us on a walk through the woods. "Daddy, what's the little plant with the red thing peeking out the top?"

"That wild flower's called Crow's Feet. Don't pick it. It's scarce around here. Let it go to seed. Next year, we'll come back and find many more Crow's Feet if we leave it."

"Moss grows on the north side of trees, girls. If you ever get lost in the woods, look for the moss."

Dad pointed at a shiny leaf plant, "That's poison ivy. Remember how it looks and stay away from it."

"That's a cottonwood tree. And that tree's a mulberry. Over there's a silver maple. See how the wind is blowing up the silver side of the leaves? That's a sure sign of rain."

"Young willow trees make the best wiener roasting sticks."

We learned Dad's method of forecasting the weather. "The cattle are restless," he would say. "Storm's brewing."

"There's a ring around the moon. It'll rain before morning."

"See the shiny spot in the sky by the sun? It's called a sun dog. That's a sign of rain in the summer or snow in the winter."

"The wooly worms are furrier this fall. Its gonna

be a hard winter.''

I was five and I couldn't whistle. Other kids my age whistled. What was wrong with my whistler? I puckered my mouth until my jaw muscles ached. When I blew through my o-shaped lips, all that came out was ''ssst.'' ''Daddy, I gotta whistle. Show me how.''

''Stick your little finger in your mouth,'' said Dad. ''now, curl your tongue and lips around your finger. Pull your finger out. Blow.''

I followed his directions. Nothing happened.

''Try it again,'' said Dad.

I tried again. Still, nothing happened.

''This time don't blow so hard,'' said Dad.

I didn't. I didn't make any sound either.

For weeks, my whistler failed to work. Finally, a feeble ''tweet'' came from between my puckered lips. I had whistled! Everyone at home cheered. My wailing to whistle was over. But my wailing whistle had only begun.

Any six-year-old should be able to snap fingers. I was six and my fingers wouldn't snap. Frustrating days followed. My right thumb and middle finger ached. Blisters raised on the fingertips.

''Daddy, why can't I snap my fingers like you?'' I asked.

''Practice, Nancy. It takes practice.''

''I **am** practicing.''

''Good. You'll get the hang of it sooner or later.''

Dad was right. I got the hang of it much later. Then came left hand learning.

Linda and I didn't learn much about housework. Mother encouraged us to go outside and help Dad. ''He doesn't have any boys,'' said Mom. ''He needs your help more than I do.'' Once said, Mom didn't have to repeat it. We were out the door after Dad in two seconds flat.

Weeds in the soybean field meant money in our pockets. Dad gave us a sharp hoe and said, ''Get all the weeds, girls. I'll pay you fifty cents an hour.'' We walked up one bean row and down another in the hot summer sun hoeing up horse weeds, cockle burrs, velvet leafs, milk weeds, button weeds, and stink weeds.

A neighbor hired Linda and me to clean weeds out of his soybean field. ''What does your Dad pay you?'' He asked.

''Fifty cents an hour,'' said Linda.

''I'll pay you seventy-five cents an hour,'' said our nice neighbor.

''Great.'' Linda and I shouted in unison.

We soon discovered that working for him at

seventy-five cents an hour wasn't so great. In his bean field, he grew more weeds than beans. It would've been easier to hoe out the beans instead of the weeds. But Linda and I went to work on his weed field and cleaned out the crop of weeds. It took us four hot, sun-baked days. Another lesson learned. After that, we looked over a bean field before we agreed to clean out the weeds.

Dad baled alfalfa hay three times each summer. He hired hay hands to handle bales in the field and at the barn. "Girls, will you see that the hay hands have all the food and water they want whenever they want it?" asked Dad. Would we! The hay hands were all boys not much older than we. We drove the tractor and pulled hay sleds from field to barn and back all day long.

On a scorching day in July, the sky clouded over. Hay hands had left until the next day. Dad jumped on the tractor with an empty hay sled hooked behind it. "Come on, girls. We've got to get the hay in the barn before it rains." The race was on between man and mother nature.

Linda and I were playing with the neighbor kids. "Can they go with us," we asked. "I guess so. Climb on the sled. Hurry!"

Linda and I jumped onto the hay sled. The neighbor kids followed. Dad took off for the hay field. In the field, I drove the tractor while Dad stacked bales twelve long, six high, and two deep on the sled. Neighbor kids and Linda ran all over the field. Thunder rumbled and lightning flashed in the western sky as the storm clouds rolled in over the tree tops behind our house.

Dad climbed on the tractor and all eight of us kids scrambled on top of the load of hay for a joy ride across the stubble to the barn. At the end of the field, Dad turned the tractor toward the barn. Unfortunately, we kids didn't lean into the turn. Bales of hay began to slip and tumble in slow motion. One hundred forty-four bales and eight kids tobbled to the ground. Hay chaff stung our eyes, clung to our hair, and filled our mouths.

Dad shut off the tractor and ran back to the pile of people and hay. He helped us struggle out of the bales and brush ourselves off. "Everybody okay?" asked Dad.

"I think so," I replied. "Wait! I count only seven of us. Where's baby Brendy?" We frantically pushed bales aside and called, "Brendy! Brendy!"

At last, Linda found the two-year-old. She sat on the ground wiping her eyes while two bales of hay formed a tepee over her head. We all sighed a sigh of relief, hugged Brendy, then cleaned hay chaff from her hair.

"Hurry. All of you," Dad instructed. "Help me load up this hay again. It's gonna rain any second!"

All of us tackled the scattered bales. We pushed, shoved and heaved them to Dad. He re-stacked them onto the sled. As we finished loading, giant rain drops fell on our heads. Dad leaped onto the tractor. "I'll put the hay in the barn. You kids run to the house. Nobody's riding!" We ran. Dad got the hay in the barn before the downpour. For once, Mother Nature was patient and kind. Dad won the race against her coming rain.

The four of us worked side by side many hours a day. Our most terrible togetherness task was the once a year toilet trench clean-out. The mere thought of it made by skin crawl. There was no way out of the job. "Put on your oldest clothes today," Dad would tell us. "We're cleaning out the toilet." Oldest clothes were a must. We would burn them after the job was done.

Dad hooked the manure spreader behind the tractor and pulled it to the toilet. "Come on, girls. Help me push the toilet over onto its side." We pushed the toilet over. The dug out trench lay exposed to air and elements giving off an unde-scribable stench.

Dad passed out shovels. "Let's get to work. We ain't got all day." Each of us stuck in our shovel, scooped up a load, and heaved it into the spreader. The trick was to work as fast as possible without breathing. It was not enjoyable, but nobody ever became ill or died from the work.

As a small child, I was afraid of the dark. I trembled under the covers in my bed at night. Outside, a giant circled our house. I heard his footsteps; thump-thump, thump-thump. The more frightened I became the faster he stomped around the house. Many anxious nights went by before I found out who made that sound. It was my own heart pounding in fright.

On a dark night, I woke up thirsty. Everyone else was asleep. I crawled out of bed and felt my way into the dark living room and on to the kitchen. I drank water from the dipper in the bucket on the dry sink. All was still, inside the house and out. I felt my way back into the living room and headed for the bedroom. "RAAAAHHHHH!" Something roared. It grabbed me from behind. I screamed and screamed. A full sixty seconds passed before I stopped screaming. It woke everyone in the house—except Dad. He was the "something" that had grabbed me from behind after he roared.

Following that fright, I refused to get up alone in the night until we installed electric lights. Then I crept out of bed, leaned against the bedroom door casing, and reached for the living room lightswitch on the other side of the wall. With a light on, I moved cautiously to the kitchen door and repeated a light switch search. Electricity to light the night made life less frightening when a dad lurked in the dark corners of the house.

"I want to learn how to play the piano," I said again and again. Finally, when I was ten, Mom and Dad invested in an old piano. Lessons began. My piano teacher said, "Practice."

I did—when I felt like it. Mom shook her head over the sticky situation. "My mother made me practice for nine long years," she said. "I'm not going to stand over you with a stick, Nancy. You're on your own."

When I did sit down at the piano, I played music any way but the correct way. Dad explained my piano learning in one sentence. "No matter what the piece, Nancy plays it boogie woogie." Mom endured my spasmodic boogie woogie as long as she could. After two years, she finally said, "no more piano lessons, Nancy. I'm not paying seventy-five cents a week for lessons when you won't practice."

Linda and I learned valuable lessons from Mom: "Wear clean underwear when you go anywhere, girls. You never know when you might be in an accident."

"Say please and thank you, girls. Politeness pays."

"And don't spend all your money. It's bad to be broke on a rainy day."

We learned from Dad's arithmetic problems. "If I had four apples and gave you one, how many would I have left?" asked Dad.

"Three," said Linda. "Now it's Nancy's turn."

"If I had three pigs, you had one pig, Nancy, and Linda had two pigs, how many pigs would we have?" asked Dad.

"Six. Why did Linda have one more pig than me?"

"Never mind. Here's a hard one. If you looked down the road and saw four tractors followed by five cars, one school bus, three trucks, a horse and buggy, and seven bicycles, what would you have?"

"Four tractors plus five cars are nine plus one school bus equals ten plus—plus—I give up. What would I have?

"A road full!"

Saturday night meant movie time. Dad took the four of us to the Grand Theater in Sullivan.

Mother insisted that Linda and I lie down on Saturday afternoon. We fought naps. But Mom's rule was: no nap, no movie.

Linda and I bounced on the bed. When Mom peeked in to see if we were resting, we lay still, closed our eyes, and breathed deeply. We sure fooled Mom—or did we? Half of the time we fell asleep while pretending; the remainder of the time we lay still and rested. Mom won the nap battle after all.

At the movies, Mother cared for Linda. Dad handled me.

"Daddy, I want a drink of water."

"Okay, Nancy. Come on. There's a fountain in the lobby."

Back at our seats, I whispered, "Daddy, buy me some popcorn."

"Come with me," said Dad. "You can pay for it."

Fifteen minutes later, I whispered, "Daddy, I need another drink."

"Not now. You'll have to wait until after the show," he would whisper back.

"I can't wait. I want it now."

"If I take you out one more time, you're not

14
Saturday Night
At The Movies

coming back to see the rest of the show."

"I want a drink now."

"Okay, but I warned you."

I drank from the fountain in the lobby. "Let's go back in, Daddy."

"No. We'll wait in the car until Mommy comes out with Linda after the show."

"But I'll miss the cartoons."

"That's right. You knew that when I brought you out for a drink."

"Please, Daddy. I like cartoons. Please?"

"No, Nancy. And that's final."

Another lesson learned and remembered. I didn't stop saying, "I want a drink," or "I want popcorn," at the movies, but when Dad finally said, "If I take you out you're not coming back.", I shut my mouth and saw the rest of the show.

Westerns were our favorite movies. Roy Rogers and Trigger, Rex Allen and Koko, or Gene Autry and Champion were our heros and their horses. Our "superstars" sung their way out of danger or fired pearl-handled six-guns twenty times before reloading. At the end of the movie they and their leading ladies rode off into the black and white sunset singing songs of love; or hid kisses behind their white hats. The heros' horses were their help-mates. Those critters did everything but speak their masters' lines and sing their songs.

If a hero needed help to sing his way out of trouble, he called on the Sons of the Pioneers with their "tumbling, tumbling weeds." Sidekicks Gabby (Hayes), Cookie (Devine), or Smiley (Burnett) helped our heroes smile.

All week long, Linda and I waited for Saturday night to see the next shoot out. "I wouldn't be in a movie if I couldn't have the part of a cowgirl with a horse," said Linda. For once, I agreed with her.

"When I was a boy," said Dad, "I wanted to see a fight between Tom Mix and Buck Jones."

Linda and I stared at Dad. "Who were they?"

"You don't know—? Oh, yeah. Before your time. They were cowboy movie stars when I was your age."

Movies amused Linda and me. Their fantasies (in black and white) delighted our imaginations. At home, we daydreamed in living color of Hollywood's excitement and adventure.

Throughout the summer of 1952, the village of Bruce showed free movies every Thursday night. After dark, the empty pasture west of the little grocery store became an outdoor theater. Black and white pictures flashed across a wrinkled sheet-screen strung between two idle telephone poles. We kids sat on blankets front row center under the screen. Our parents climbed into each other's cars and visited while children howled, hissed, or hurried to the grocery store for bubble gum, soda pop, and pointed ice cream cones.

Dad didn't buy a television until I was fourteen and Linda was ten. What did we do before TV? We looked at one another and carried on sensible conversations. Room arrangements were balanced; not one ugly television on the far side of the room and all the chairs lined along the opposite wall. When we walked across the room no one yelled, "Get out of my way!" or "You make a better door than a window."

Our neighbor had a television. The picture was small and round when it could be seen. Most of the time our neighbor didn't watch a picture on the screen: He watched snow.

We had a radio in the living room. It was four feet tall, three feet wide and one foot deep. Why was it so big? To hold the man who talked inside, naturally.

We finished supper by half-past six every weekday evening. Linda and I jumped up from the table and dashed to the radio. We wouldn't think of missing The Lone Ranger's "Hi,Ho, Silver!" and Tonto's "Get'um up Scout." On alternate nights, either Sky King, cowboy pilot or Sargent Preston of the Yukon was on the radio after the Lone Ranger program.

Before the time of television in every home, Mom's Aunt Carrie invited us over for New Year's Day dinner in front of their television. The black and white console temporarily sat on a raised wooden platform. (All the better to see the Rose Bowl parade on the screen from a back row seat.)

Six rows of five chairs each were lined up from one end of the living room to the other facing the television. Every man, woman, and child filled their plates and ate in the living room while they watched the snowy picture of parading floats and pounding football players.

Country telephones offered entertainment not equaled in movies, radio, or television. We shared a party line with eight other families. Our brown wooden box hung on a wall in the hall. On the box, two black round bells were eyes, a mouthpiece was the nose, and a shelf formed the mouth. On the right side of the telephone was a crank. The receiver hung on the left side.

Our telephone number was Kirksville 515 on 11:

one long ring, one short ring, and one long ring called us to answer the telephone. If the telephone sounded a long, everyone in the house stopped what they were doing and waited. Who was the call for? It might be Stephens' (their ring was one long, two shorts) or Simms' (their ring was one long, three shorts). Maybe it was for Perrings (their ring was one long, one short, one long, one short). Waiting out that ring took patience. More than once I almost answered the telephone before the last short ring.

Four longs meant emergency. Every party liner raised his receiver and heard, "Allens' barn's on fire!" or "Rugbys' house is burning!" or "There'll be a telephone meeting at the switchboard in Kirksville tomorrow afternoon at three."

Through the party line, we heard news of our neighbors. One long, three shorts came the ring. "Listen in on that, Nancy," said Mom. "Find out how Mrs. Simm's mother is after her operation."

One long, one short, one long, one short shrilled through the house. "I'll listen to that," Mom told us.

"Maybe Mrs. Perring had her baby. It's due."

Dad came in and asked, "Have you listened to any of Bascins's calls today?"

"No."

"Well, do if it rings. That looks like Doctor Swain's car parked in their drive."

To make a call, I lifted off the earpiece, put it against my left ear, and listened. The line was clear. With my left hand holding the earpiece, I pushed down the holder and turned the crank with my right hand. One long ring called central or operator. When central answered, I said, "Sullivan 4632, please" or "Bruce 9 on 14." As I waited for the call to go through, I heard line popping, receiver clicking, and cross talk.

Enough of entertainment country style. After the coming of television, Saturday night at the movies for the entire family became a thing of the past, along with theater crying rooms for children, twenty-five cent tickets and ten cent popcorn.

We had cats galore: often more than twenty-four. Motorboat was our tiger-colored cat named for her powerful purr. On a spring afternoon, Linda found Motorboat in a box on the back porch. She had four new baby kittens.

Linda ran for me. "Nancy! Come and see Motorboat. She has four new babies!" We hurried back to the box. Motorboat didn't have four kittens, she had five. Then six. Seven. Eight! Right before our very eyes. Motorboat outdid herself and all the other mama cats on our farm.

Linda and I didn't teach our cats any tricks. We tried but they wouldn't cooperate. We couldn't even teach them to come when we called their names. Dad said the cats were too proud to do silly stunts. Linda and I decided stubborn was a better word for the cats' personalities. Our cats had minds of their own. They wanted their way; not our way.

We stood in the back yard and called, "Here Boots. Here Sox. Here Mustard, Midnight, Patches, and Blue. Come here, Tiger. Here Gidget, Puff, Snowball, Matilda, and Sue. Here Petunia. Here Beulah." (To name a few.) No cat came to the call of his or her name.

Linda and I hit on an idea. We named the next

15
Parade Of Pets

cat Kitty. Kitty responded to her name. She came every time we called her. All we had to do was say, "Here Kitty, Kitty, Kitty." She came running—so did twenty other cats.

We played with doll clothes; on cats not dolls. Dressing a wiggly black cat in a pink bonnet and pinafore was much more challenging than putting clothes on a stiff-legged doll whose eyes were her only moveable parts.

Two dogs at a time guarded our farm and gave us love. Our dogs were our best friends. In addition to being playmates, they protected our property including Dad's tank of tractor gas.

Spot grew old and feeble. He hobbled from his feed bowl to his bed on the back porch rarely venturing any farther away. His left hind leg was gone. The tractor mower amputated it on a day when Dad was in the field mowing.

Late one afternoon, a neighbor stopped in front of the house, "Dale, I think that's your spotted dog laying in the road a half mile back. Looks like a car hit him."

"Is he dead?" asked Dad.

" 'Fraid so."

"Thanks, Slim. The girls and I'll bury him."

Linda and I jumped into the truck to go pick up Spot. "Oh, boy. We can get a new puppy now," I proclaimed. "Spot was so old and grouchy." Linda agreed.

Then we saw Spot laying in the road ahead of us. Spot was quite dead. A lump swelled up in my throat. Tears stung my eyes. Linda cried, along with me. Spot had grown old and grouchy but earlier in the day he had tried to romp and play with us. We would miss our poor old dog.

Dad dug a grave and buried Spot behind the barn. Linda and I marked the site with a wooden cross.

Cutie missed Spot. When Spot died, Cutie became number one dog. He was a tri-colored collie-type dog standing eighteen inches tall.

Cutie may have been little but he was mighty. He wasn't afraid of anything. "Let's teach Cutie to be a mouser and a ratter," said Dad. "Bring him to the corn crib, Nancy. When I scoop out the corn today, mice and rats will run everywhere."

I tied a rope around Cutie's neck and led him to the corn crib. In the crib, Cutie and I watched Dad scoop corn. I was scared. I didn't want any mouse or rat darting up my pant legs. I tucked the legs of my pants into my gum boots and kept my eyes wide open.

"There's a mouse," shouted Dad. "Get him,

Cutie!"

I joined in. "Go get him, Cutie! Don't let him get away!"

Cutie understood. He caught the fleeing mouse and killed it with one bite of his jaws. Afterwards, I hugged our little dog around the neck and said, "Good boy, Cutie. You're the greatest."

Moments later, Dad yelled, "There's one! There's one!"

"Go, Cutie," I shouted. Cutie hesitated. I pulled him to the spot Dad indicated. We didn't find a mouse. We found a snake. I dashed outside to get as far away from that snake as possible. Dad's laugh rang out behind me.

In front of the corn crib door, I sat down on the ground and shook. Then it happened. Something long and round landed on the ground beside me—the snake. Dad had thrown it out. I screamed, then was mad. "Dad, you threw that snake at me on purpose," I accused.

When Dad finally stopped laughing, he told me, "I swear I didn't know you were sitting on the ground in front of the door."

Did he or didn't he? I would never know for sure. But I did know that if he wanted Cutie to be a mouser or a ratter (not to mention a snaker), Dad

would have to teach the dog **all by himself**.

Cutie specialized in dog fights all his life. He chose opponents twice his size and won every fight until his last one. It proved to be the death of him. He was ten when I was fourteen. Cutie crawled home from a notorious fight. He had lost his first match. Mud caked his black hair, one eye had

been torn away and an ear was missing. His spirit was defeated. He had lost the battle and soon lost his life.

Dad dug a grave next to Spot's resting place and buried Cutie beside his old friend who had gone before him. Linda and I marked Cutie's grave with another wooden cross.

Ted had joined our family after Spot's death. He became number two puppy when Cutie moved to number one. Linda was five and I was nine when a wild dog gave birth to five brown puppies in Grandpa and Grandma Hogue's corn crib a quarter-mile behind their house. Six weeks later, when the mother dog went hunting, Dad, Linda, and I sneaked into the crib, trapped Ted, and took him home. He was brown, grew tall, and had medium long hair.

As time went by, Linda and I taught Ted to shake hands, play dead, roll over, jump hurdles, hoops, and hedges, plus red wagon riding (to Mother's distress).

Ted was a happy dog. He smiled. Anytime we came back after being away Ted greeted us with his curled upper lip smiling from ear to ear.

Ted talked, when he wasn't smiling. "Ted, say hungry," coaxed Linda. Ted opened his mouth. His lower jaw quivered as he mouthed the word.

Finally, he said, "Arr-ry."

"Good dog. Now say hamburger, Ted. Hamburger."

More mouth quivering, then, "Arrm-burr-grr."

Dad joined in our conversation, "Say eat, Ted. Eat."

"Err."

"Good dog. Now say hello."

"Errr-o."

We were delighted with our speaking dog. He was delighted with our treats, pats and attention.

Ted disappeared when he was four years old. One night he was there, the next morning he was gone. Long, sad days followed Ted's disappearance. Linda and I searched for his body along road sides and in the timber. Dad questioned farmers for miles around. He learned that three neighbors had lost their big, healthy dogs at the same time. They, too, had no clue. Were dog nappers at work? We never knew.

Five days later at the supper table, Dad said, "Okay, girls. Chins up. Time to get another dog." A friend of a friend gave Dad one of his almost-purebred collie pups. We named our new pet Lad.

Lad didn't replace our memory of Ted. He made his own niche in our hearts. Ted wasn't forgotten, but sadness faded away. The pleasure of reminiscing about Ted's four years of tricks shone brightly through the years.

Lad grew into a responsible "cow dog" as well as our lovable sable and white collie playmate.

"Fetch the cows, Lad," commanded Dad. Lad loped away into the dense timber behind the house. Before long, he came running with the herd of cattle. That in itself was not unique, but how he did it was.

Lad nosed out the grazing cattle. He barked and nipped at them until they became angry and chased him. Lad ran to the house fast enough to stay just ahead of the thundering herd. It worked every time. It also looked far safer than herding behind heavy-hooved cattle.

Lad learned to shake hands, play dead, and roll over for our food and affection. But he didn't ride, smile, or talk. We tried to teach him but he was too busy for such nonsense.

Our dogs and cats spent their hot summer afternoons stretched out in the cool dirt beneath the house. They disappeared under the house through two holes in the old brick foundation. Linda and I followed them. We bellied our way through the cool dirt and pulled our prone bodies along with our forearms. It was a great place to play with our pets if we ignored the spiders, webs, and low ceilings.

"Daddy, buy us some rabbits, please," Linda and I begged. Finally, he agreed to buy Linda a black rabbit and me a white one. We named the bunnies Pepper and Salt, our original flavors. We helped Dad build a pen for them; then stood back and waited for babies. They didn't come. All those rabbits did was fight and bite. Dad borrowed a neighbor's white buck rabbit. Still, no babies came. The white buck rabbit joined in the battle and made it a three-way fight.

"That's it. They've gotta go," Dad informed us. He looked puzzled. Dad gave the rabbits away never knowing if they were male or female. With rabbits, it's hard to tell.

Linda and I found an abandoned baby squirrel beneath a tree in the chicken lot. Linda named him Perry. I made a nest on the back porch. "Don't bring that squirrel in the house," warned Mother. Then she cuddled the poor baby and gave us the good heating pad to keep him warm. We heat-padded Perry's nest. On chilly nights, his pad ran on low control.

We took turns feeding Perry on the back porch. He adapted to a doll's baby bottle full of milk without delay. For one week, we fed Perry by day and warmed him with a heat pad by night. The eighth night was chilly. We forgot to turn on Perry's pad. The next morning, Perry was dead from exposure.

Dad always said, "Pets can teach as well as be taught. No pet wants to do anything for a gruff voice or rough handling. Give an animal loving patience, kindness, and praise. He'll be your friend forever." Linda and I tried to follow Dad's sound advice.

Mom found a raccoon in her scrub bucket on the side porch. "Can we keep it?" we asked. "We'll make him into a pet."

Mom answered us by chasing him away with a broom.

"Daddy, will you catch us a crow and slit his tongue for us? We want to teach him to talk."

"There's enough talking around here. We don't need to add an old crow."

"Daddy, we want a pet skunk. "Will you catch one for us?"

"Not on your life. You two stinkers are enough for me."

Needless to say, we settled for mostly cats and mainly dogs in our parade of pets.

Dad's a Democrat. So was his father before him and his father before him. "Always vote for a Democrat," said Dad. "They're for the little people, like us farmers. Republicans are for big business. They don't care about small business."

"When you don't know the candidate personally, vote for the Democratic Party. Hoover was a Republican president. He got us into the Great Depression of the thirties. Now take Franklin Roosevelt. There was a president! He was a Democrat. The American people elected him to the White House four times!"

"Did you go to the second World War," asked Linda.

"No but I was called up once. The draft board wanted me to hire an older man to farm the land while I was gone. I said I'd have to sell instead. So, they sent me home to farm my land and help feed the nation."

"Did anyone from Sullivan go to war?" I asked.

"Yes. Almost every young man who was healthy and didn't farm. My brother Earl tried to join the army but they didn't send him overseas. They sent him home. Earl weighed three hundred and fifty pounds. The army said they could send two one hundred and seventy-five pound men in his place."

16
Always Vote For A Democrat

"During the war everyone raised victory gardens," said Mom. "We didn't call ours a victory garden because we always raised food whether there was a war going on or not."

"Why were they called victory gardens?"

"Food and supplies were scarce—there were hardly enough to go around. We had to have coupons to buy sugar from 1942 to 1947. Our ration of sugar was more than we ever used. Coffee was rationed, too. But your dad and I didn't drink coffee then."

"Was anything else hard to get?" I asked.

"Sure," said Dad. "Gas was rationed. But I had enough to do the farming. We didn't drive much in the 1941 Ford. Not because of lack of gas but because we couldn't buy tires. And we couldn't buy a new car. I signed up for a new Ford in May of 1945 and didn't get it until August of 1948."

"Gosh," said Linda. "Couldn't anybody buy a car?"

"Not if he was honest. Some people got cars and machinery off the black market. The black market sold rationed goods secretly at high prices during the war. It was against the law because the government had set price ceilings on rationed goods."

"Did you buy anything in the black market?"

"No. No patriotic American bought through the black market. Besides, the cost of black market goods was sky high."

Truman was a good Democrat, too, Dad thought. "He looked out for the farmers. He even had milk poured down hillsides to keep up milk prices. And, he had the Korean conflict to worry about."

I knew a little about the Korean conflict. I had overheard a cousin tell Dad about his experiences while fighting in Korea. My eleven-year-old imagination ran wild down the path of fears in my mind. For two weeks, I had terrible dreams of bombing followed by invading soldiers with bayonets on the end of their rifles. I visualized them hiding in the hayloft, lurking behind the storm cellar, and stalking in the hen house.

I worried, fretted and stewed; but told no one. At noon on the fifteenth day, the sky above our house filled with roaring airplanes. From somewhere in the distance, I heard a terrific boom, then another, and another. It was happening. First the bombing; next the invastion. I fled into the house, crouched in the stairwell closet and trembled with fear. Mother found me there. "What's the matter?"

"B-bombing. Soldiers come next," I stammered

through chattering teeth.

"Oh, Nancy," said Mother. She drew me out of the closet and folded her arms around me. "The explosions you heard were supersonic booms caused by fast jets breaking through the sound barrier. Listen. The roaring planes are gone. They're hundreds of miles away by now. Probably already to an air force base somewhere. Tell me your problem." I related my fears to Mom. In facing them logically, they were no longer frightening.

On with the presidents. Dad thought Eisenhower didn't do anything but smile and play golf. "That's a Republican for you," said Dad. "If Stevenson had been elected, things would've been better. Stevenson wore a pair of shoes until there were holes in the soles. He had to be a thrifty man to do that."

It made no difference who was president, Mom and Dad had to struggle to make ends meet.

Dad learned how to install electrical wiring. He made extra money wiring old houses and barns for electricity after the Rural Electrical Association strung electric wires on poles by farms in the sticks.

Mom and Dad also hung wallpaper to add to their income. Mom slapped on the paste; Dad hung up the paper.

One day, they hung wallpaper for an old friend of Dad's parents, Ott. Linda and I went with Mom and Dad on this job. Big, old, grey-haired Ott knew us. "He can tolerate the girls," said Dad when Mom worried.

Linda was two. She puddled in the middle of the kitchen floor. Ott cleaned it up. "Don't stop Wilma," said Ott in his deep gruff voice. "Keep on pastin'."

I washed my hands in the bathroom and overflowed the sink. Ott cleaned it up. "Don't stop Wilma," he said. "Keep on pastin'."

Ott fixed dinner for all of us. We sat around his kitchen table. Ott carried a bowl of hot gravy to the table and set it down beside my plate. He eased into the chair next to mine and passed the mashed potatoes. Then he picked up the gravy. My chewing gum stuck to the gravy bowl, the table, and his hands. I'll be damned," was all Ott said.

I shrank down in my chair. Mom jumped up. "Don't stop, Mr. Seemore," she said. "Go on eating."

While Mom cleaned off chewing gum, Dad and Ott laughed at the mess. Mom, Linda and I didn't see anything funny. But then we didn't know that Ott's gruff was worse than his gripe.

Even with extra jobs along the way, Dad had to borrow money from the bank to operate on. If during the borrowing season, I wanted a new dress or shoes, Mom stopped my requests with the words, "We can't buy it with borrowed money. Wait until we get the crops out in the fall." I waited.

When I was growing up, I knew we didn't have much money, but no one ever said we were poor. To me, we never were. We had much more than money could buy.

Dad worried about money. If he bought a new tractor, he worried about it and lost sleep for at least three nights afterwards. The same thing happened if he bought a car, a chair, or a coat. Mom covered old chairs, patched coats, and kept accurate books. She couldn't talk Dad out of worrying so she pinched pennies to the extreme.

Dad voted Democratic. Mom voted the way he told her to. Dad also said, "A penny saved is a penny earned." But he didn't say, "Don't worry about tomorrow. Let tomorrow take care of itself." Mom said that.

Dad was too busy worrying about tomorrow.

Dad and Mom knew their neighbors who lived near by or farther away. They neighborly neighbored to any neighbor's need in the neighborhood.

A farming neighbor who lived three miles away was gored by a bull. His left leg was broken, two ribs were cracked, and stitches held his side together. Unfortunately it was time to cultivate his crops. Like farmers have done for years, Dad and nine other neighbors dropped what they were doing for a day and took their tractors with mounted cultivators to the less fortunate neighbor's fields. All day, ten tractors tilled one hundred fifty acres of green corn and soybeans. They made one short stop for lunch served by their wives. By sundown the task was done. None of the ten volunteers expected anything in return. Their reward was in being a good neighbor.

Two of our neighbors were borrowers. Dad didn't mind borrowers unless the exception became the rule. It sometimes did. One neighbor was known as the machinery borrower. He borrowed a well-oiled field rake or wagon and brought it back bent or squeaky dry. A second neighbor was the bull borrower. He didn't mend his half of the pasture fence; therefore, Dad's bull got into the

17
Know Your Neighbors

neighbor's cows. The bull borrower raised hereford calves every year without ever buying a bull for his cows.

When Dad and Mom finally caught up with their work, we all jumped into the car and rode around the neighborhood.

"Look at Fred's corn rows," Dad would point. "They're as crooked as a dog's hind leg."

"Can't you get more seed in a crooked row, Daddy?"

Dad chuckled. "Maybe so. But I always work hard to make my rows as straight and neat as I can."

Dad became the "historical" ride guide. We were his attentive audience. "See the tumbled-down shack back in that field?" We saw it. "That's where Dewy Hand lived until he died. Richest man in these parts and he lived in that shack for twenty years all by himself."

Farther down the oiled road, Dad said, "There's the house where old man Marten lived. Summer or winter, he sat in his chair on the sagging front porch and rocked all day long. He was the oldest man I ever knew. Died when he was a hundred and two."

One mile later, Dad said, "There's where Levi Lanum lived. His boy was kicked in the head by a horse. Doctor said he was dead. They laid him out on his bed like folks did when I was young. His ma sat up with the body all night. Early next morning, relatives heard her scream. They dashed to the bedroom. There was the boy sitting on the edge of the bed. He wasn't dead at all. Just unconscious. But after the fright, his ma near died."

Dad drove the car around a curve. "That sagging building used to be the Quigley general store. I remember the time Dad, Earl, and I bought fifty head of cattle in Stewardson and drove them up this road. We stopped at that windmill for a drink then drove them twenty-four miles home."

We came to Dad's home place. He pointed left. "Back there in the cornfield was where we had the horse barn that was struck by lightning. It burned to the ground with Bess and Nell inside. Remember me telling you about them? They were the biggest and best work horses I ever farmed with."

We remembered but we were always ready for Dad to tell us one of his stories one more time. "Tell us, Daddy. Tell us about Bess and Nell!" He never failed to fulfill our requests.

Our neighbor to the east was part Indian and proud of it. His nickname was Apache. Dad and Apache got into a dispute over boundary lines. Dad suggested surveyors. Apache refused. Dad measured on his own. Apache didn't trust Dad's measurements.

One evening Dad looked up and saw Apache stomping up the drive toward us in the front yard. "Oh ho, girls," whispered Dad. "Here comes Chief-Rain-in-the-Face. He's on the warpath again." Dad strolled out to meet Apache.

Linda darted ahead of Dad and questioned, "Apache, are you Chief-Rain-in-the-Face on the warpath? Daddy says you are."

Apache flushed beet red with rage. He turned tail and stomped home. Dad didn't find out what he had come for because Apache didn't speak to Dad for several months. When he finally spoke again, he was a peaceful man.

In 1953, a mentally disturbed man killed his favorite cousin in Mattoon. Two hours later, his car was found abandoned at the river bridge three miles from our house. State police alerted the neighborhood. The manhunt began. Linda carried a wooden ball bat on her shoulder for three days. Day and night, the bat went with her to the table, in the car, behind the house. I stayed close to Linda and her deadly bat. On the third day authorities found the suspect's body floating face down in the Kaskaskia river. All neighbors sighed a sigh of relief—and a sigh of sadness.

A drought scorched the countryside during the summer of 1954. Parched days soared to temperatures of 110 degrees. One Sunday evening the odor of burning wood filled our nostrils. Smoke hung heavy about our house. "Fire somewhere," said Dad. "Could be our timber. Go on inside. I'll drive around and see what's burning."

Mother, Linda, and I went into the house and waited—and waited—and waited. Dad didn't come home. At length, Mom sent us to bed. She appeared calm but I knew she had to be as concerned as Linda and I were.

The next morning when I awoke the smell of burnt wood still hung in the air. I heard Dad talking to Mom at the kitchen table. At last, he was home. I dashed down the stairs in time to hear him say, "A thousand acres burned over by Red Fox school about five miles southwest of here. Lots of neighbors and I fought the flames all night. It's out now. The backfire finally worked."

"What about all the wild animals?" I asked.

"They ran. Squirrels, rabbits, 'coons, 'possums, skunks, foxes—all the animals headed for the river. If they made it to the other side, they were safe.

The fire didn't cross the river. We were mighty worried. Thank God the wind died."

Two days later, Dad drove us to the scene of destruction. Mounds of charred tree trunks still smouldered on the otherwise barren landscape. Blackened poles stood where full-leafed trees had rustled in the breeze seventy-two hours before. The earth was black to gray as far as our eyes could see. The stench of burned death lingered over the land. An unattended trash fire had started the eventual massacre of trees and animals. No man lost his life. Every man lost years of God's beauty.

"Know your neighbors," said Mother and Dad, and let your neighbors know you."

Our Christmas at home overflowed with anticipated excitement. Santa Claus led the way to wishing Jesus a happy birthday.

Our house didn't have a fireplace for Santa to slide down on Christmas Eve. I was concerned. To add to my worry, Dad built up the fire in the coal stoves until perspiration popped out. He looked my way and said, "That should keep Santa from coming down the chimney this year."

"He can come through the door," I countered.

"Nope. I locked all the doors. Now off to bed. Santa won't get in this year."

Dad didn't keep Santa out. Somehow, he got inside. Bright and early Christmas morning, Linda and I found peanuts in the shell overflowing from our shoes. Oranges filled our stockings. Toys crowded around the Christmas tree. Santa was a tricky one at our house. He knew how to pick locks, Or, was it an inside job?

One Christmas morning, Santa left footprints in the soft blanket of new fallen snow on our front lawn. Linda and I followed his tracks which led up to the house and back to the road. Sled marks dented the fresh snow covering the road. We saw them—Dad pointed them out to us. An orange lay beside the footprints. Santa had dropped it in his

18
Was Santa Daddy ? Or Was Daddy Santa ?

haste. That's what Dad said.

One week before each Christmas day, Dad picked up a spade and bucket then said, "Time to find our Christmas tree, girls." We bundled up and followed Dad into the timber. Through valleys and over hills, we searched for an evergreen tree just the right size to fit on a stool before the front room window. At last, we found one. Linda held the bucket, I held the tree, Dad dug it up. He put the tree roots into the bucket and packed dirt around it. Back to the house we marched with our Christmas tree in tow.

In the front room, Dad set the transplanted tree on the stool before the window. All evening long the four of us strung popcorn and cranberries to drape on the tree. We punched holes in homemade cut-out cookies, tied string through the holes and hung them on the tree limbs. A strand of colorful lights were strung about the tree making it glow with red, yellow, blue, and green hues.

After Christmas, Dad would plant our tree in the yard to grow for another year. Birds would come and eat popcorn, cranberries, and cookies from the branches.

Gifts should be appreciated for the portion of the person wrapped inside, if not for the present. Mother reminded Linda and me of that every Christmas. Mother's Aunt Lola gave us girls a present every yuletide season. It was always the same—a new pair of pretty panties—year after year. Only the color and size changed. Annually, Mother said, "We're going to Aunt Lola's. Now when you open the panties this year, think of her thoughtfulness."

It was difficult for two tomboys to put enthusiasm into the expected thank you's for "panties one more time." Mom liked the dressy panties. She gave us sound advice, so we tried our best to act surprised and look pleased.

Before my tenth Christmas, I announced to Mom and Dad, "Don't buy me any toys this year. I'm too big for them."

"Not even one?" asked Mother.

"No. That's baby stuff. I want a train case, clothes, and things like that."

"All right. But I don't like it," said Dad. "Can't Santa leave you one toy?"

"No. I've outgrown toys."

On Christmas morning, Linda tore into her gifts. She had a doll, an electric train, two wind-up animals, and trinkets. I opened my gifts; a blue train case, new red jeans, a cardigan sweater, and a hand mirror. No toys. No games. No trinkets.

I went to the bathroom and cried because I didn't get any unwanted toys. Ultimately, I dried my tears, washed my face, and walked out of the bathroom wearing a ghost of a grin. I tried to conceal my desire for toys. I liked my presents. But maybe I wasn't as grown up as I'd thought I was. (Fifteen years later, I learned that my attempt at concealment had been in vain. Mother and Dad were discussing Christmas gifts for **my** three children. Mother said to me, "What about toys? Remember the Christmas you cried when you didn't get any toys even though it was your idea?" I was speechless. How did she know?)

January one was the holiday when Dad said, "Watch out for today. What ever you do, you'll do it all year." I believed him and proceeded with caution.

We spent most of New Year's Day visiting. Dad would have us visit grandpas and grandmas and aunts and uncles. "We want to start the new year off right."

April Fool's Day was planned in earnest beneath our roof. At the crack of dawn, Dad said to us, "There's a spot on your chin." Or, "What's that on your nose?" Thus began the day to "fool the rest of the family but don't get fooled."

Dad used catsup on his fingers for blood. He ripped rags for pretend bandages. We believed him until he said, "April Fool!"

All forms of animal life were "sighted" in the yard, behind the sofa, and under the bed. As time went on, it became impossible to fool anyone around our house.

On the night of July third, we celebrated Independence Day. Dad hand-turned three freezers of ice cream. Uncles, aunts, grandparents, and cousins came to eat and watch our front yard fireworks. When it grew dark enough, Dad became the official fireworks fuse man. Ohhs and ahhs provided background music to rainbow stars bursting in the ebony skies.

Linda and I almost shared birthdays; hers being October 22nd, and mine October 24th. Each year, Mom and Dad held a birthday weiner roast for us. They invited family and friends. There was no comparison to a weiner roast in the cow pasture.

"Bring your own weiners and buns and marsh-mellows. Relishes, cocoa, donuts, and cider will be furnished." "There'll be a short hayride for the kids and coffee for the grown-ups." "Don't wear good clothes. We'll be playing hide and seek and run for your supper in the pasture." "Don't hit the electric fence. Crawl under it to get to the bonfire and weiner sticks."

Halloween was nearly forgotten on our farm. Harvest time took its place.

Thanksgiving: the special holiday to pause and praise the Lord. It was a time to celebrate the harvest and offer thanks. A farmer planted with faith. Faith in the changing seasons; from spring showers to summer sun on into fall frost and winter's snowy cover. Some may call it the ways of Mother Nature. We, in accord with the earth, recognized it as the grace of God.

Death knocked at Grandma Lane's door in July of 1954. Linda was a third grader. I was in the seventh. Dad was 38 when his mother passed away.

The last time I saw short, stout Grandma Lane, she lay in a hospital bed crunching ice to keep cool. Three nights later, she lost her long battle against the dreaded cancer attacking her stomach.

Before Grandma entered the hospital for her last stay, I went through a time of critical self-analysis. My feet were too fat; my face was too round; my body too squat; and my hands too square. The name Nancy meant full of Grace. Outside of my name, there wasn't one touch of grace in my entire body.

One Sunday afternoon, Grandma Lane patted my short, square hands between her short, square hands and said, "Look at that Nancy. Your hands are shaped exactly like mine."

From that day forward, I looked to my hands as a legacy from Grandma Lane built just right for the work they'd have to do.

Early on the morning of March fourth in 1955, the ringing telephone jarred us awake. Mom groped for the telephone, lifted the earpiece and said, "Hello" into the separate mouthpiece.

As she listened, her expression crumbled. Tears

19

A Time To Live, A Time To Die.

A Time To Laugh, A Time To Cry.

swam in her brown eyes. "We'll be right there, Mother," she choked.

Mom hung up the receiver.

"What is it, Wilma? What's the matter," asked Dad.

"It's Dad," sobbed Mom. "He had a massive stroke. The ambulance is on its way. Mother said to meet her at the hospital."

"Get dressed girls," said Dad. "You can wait for the school bus at Aunt Elsie's."

All day at school my mind returned to Grandpa Hogue again and again. How was he? Would he be all right? Could he survive another stroke?

Eleven years before, when he had been 53 years old, Grandpa suffered a disabling stroke. He had to give up farming and raising livestock as well as driving a car. Grandma drove him where ever he wanted to go. Linda and I would forever picture him in his flat, grey tweed cap with a pipe between his teeth and a curved wooden cane in his right hand. When he walked in his bibbed overalls, his left foot slid along the ground behind his right step. We didn't remember him any other way; we didn't think of him as disabled. He was our Grandpa Hogue. The walk and cane were his special trademarks.

Four days after his second stroke, Grandpa died. He never regained consciousness. He was 64 years old.

Grandma Hogue was left all alone.

For two months, she stayed with us and slept in the upstairs bedroom next to Linda's room. Two months was all Grandma could take. Thirteen was my age. Terrible was my temper. It erupted like Ole Faithful, on the hour. Living with us, Grandma became fully aware of my angry outbursts. Still, she loved me and sympathetically said, "Now, Nancy. You're not my little girl when you act that way."

One day she soothed me with the words, "Would you like to drive my car?"

Would I! I jumped behind the wheel of her last year's model Chevy. She climbed into the passenger seat beside me and said, "I'd like to go along."

Off we went down the road. Grandma patiently sat through every grind of the gears and jerk of the clutch. She didn't once raise the tone of her voice as she visited with me throughout a 'country mile' ride.

Afterwards, Dad said, "With someone trusting you as much as your Grandma, Nancy, you'll have to shape up and prove yourself trustworthy."

His advice penetrated. I strived to improve in every way.

Seven months after Grandpa Hogue's death, Grandpa Lane died of intestinal cancer. He was 69. Grandpa Lane died at home. Dad, with his brothers and sisters, took turns sitting up with Grandpa through his last, long, suffering nights.

Grandpa lost weight until he was a lengthly skeleton lying in his bed. Late one night, he passed from pain into peace.

In 15 heartbreaking months, Dad had lost both of his parents and Mother had lost her Dad. Estates were settled. Mom helped Grandma set up lonely housekeeping in a four room house in Sullivan. Their home place in the country was sold.

Grandma didn't feel well. She developed a hacking cough. The doctor diagnosed it as nerves. He prescribed shock treatments to break her out of mourning.

After shock treatments, she continued to hack and cough.

Grandma employed a live-in companion. Their personalities clashed. Grandma let her go and employed another live-in lady nearer her own age. They were compatabile. But no one could ever take Grandpa's place for Grandma.

I spent many nights at Grandma's house. If there was an after-school function, I went to Grandma's. It saved a ten mile in, ten mile out trip for Mom and Dad.

Grandma and I shared happy times visiting together in her city home.

She expected Linda and me to make good grades in school. We worked hard to earn them. After all, she approved and gave us a nickle for each A on our report cards.

In 1957, a mobil chest x-ray unit came to town. Grandma had her chest x-rayed. The report referred her to the doctor. She had a spot on her lung.

Grandma was hospitalized. Tests were taken. They came back positive. Lung cancer. Nothing could be done. Grandma went home to die.

Lung cancer was diagnosed in September. She died in December 12 days before Christmas. Grandma was 70 years old. She was no longer alone.

I was. I felt lost. At 15, I had no grandparents left. Grandma Hogue had been my last—and my favorite. My world grew blacker. I wailed hysterically at her funeral. Dad clutched my arms and drew me close. "you must not think of all the

good times you had with Grandma," he whispered. "You must think only how sick she was before she died. Then you'll make it through the funeral. Death is a state of peace and painlessness for her. Don't feel sorry for yourself. Feel safe and secure. Grandma isn't suffering. She's with God. Not in her worn out body but in her everlasting spirit."

I dwelled on Dad's words. Inner turmoil eased. Life went on. A time to die, A time to cry, touched, lingered then faded away. We moved on to a time to live, a time to laugh. Be it tomorrow or today.

20
Teen-agers
In The House

Mother set up a dish washing schedule when Linda was ten and I was fourteen. It began with morning dishes, Linda; night dishes, Nancy; switch each day. The schedule progressed smoothly until one rainy night. Dad finished the last of his chores before anyone started the night dishes. He was back indoors when Mother said, "Linda, it's your turn to wash the dishes."

"Aw, come on. Let Nancy wash," teased Dad.

"But it's Linda's turn," I retorted.

"So what. You're bigger."

That did it. I flew into a rage. "You're always trying to get Linda out of work," I yelled. "Let Nancy do it. Let Nancy do it. That's all I ever hear around here!"

"Nobody needs to help me," sighed Mother. "I'll do the dishes myself."

I wasn't satisfied. "Dad, why do you always want me doing all of the work instead of Linda?"

"I was teasing you again," said Dad. "Linda can do the dishes."

"No," said Mother. "I'll do them all by myself."

"I know when I'm not wanted around here," I cried. "I'm leaving!"

I stomped upstairs, threw clothes, brush, and comb into my suitcase, then carried it down to the back door.

Mom stood at the sink crying into the dishwater. I wasn't angry any more, I was sorry I had packed my bag. How could I get out of the "pickle" I'd put myself into this time without bursting my puffed-up pride?

Dad pulled the car keys from his pocket. "I'll drive you any place you want to go."

I gulped. A lump lodged in my throat. I gulped again. Pride's a difficult lump to swallow. "I-I don't want to go anywhere," I said. I then snatched up my suitcase and ran upstairs to hide in my room.

Later, when I strolled back down the stairs, everyone was calm and smiling. No one in our family had a long memory, it seemed. I regret to report that Mother did the dishes that day and everyday thereafter with little help from Linda or me.

When I was a freshman in high school, eleven friends came to my one and only spring snipe hunt. It all started at school when Sharon and Janet asked, "Snipe? What's a snipe?"

"They're birds you can see only at night," said Jim. They're real easy to catch. All you have to do is have two people hold a big gunny sack. The rest of the hunters surround the snipe and shoo them into the open gunny sack."

"Where are snipe?" asked Janet.

"In the timber behind my house," I said, then gulped down snickers and giggles. "I thought everyone knew about snipe hunts. Hey, why don't we have a hunt Saturday night? Sharon and Janet can catch the first ones."

Plans were made. Seven boys and four girls came that Saturday night. It grew dark. We guided Sharon and Janet deep into the timber. "Stay here. Hold the sack and whistle as if you're calling a dog. We'll circle around and drive them into the sack." Ten of us left the girls holding the bag. We circled back to the house and waited for them to see the joke and come trailing in.

We waited and waited. Sharon and Janet didn't come to the house. They got lost. We had to go trailing after them. But they were easy to find. Their loud frightened wails told us where they were.

Slumber parties brought teen-age fun among the girls thanks to patient parents who sacrificed a night's sleep by relinquishing their living room floor for our parties. Later came the pain. Lack of sleep gave us headaches. Lying on hard floors made our muscles sore. More than once, I suffered the aches of a cold after a drafty sleepless night (otherwise known as a slumber party). But we gals were always eager for the next one.

What clothes we wore in the fifties. Every night I polished my white buck shoes to wear the next day at school. None of the girls wore hose with white tie shoes. Instead we wore white tripple-rolled bobby socks and twisted or folded them until our ankles appeared swollen to twice their normal size. Why didn't we wear hose? For one thing they cost too much. For another, it was too hard to keep the black seams straight up the back of our legs all day.

At home on weekends, I soaked my three net crinolins (or can-cans) in full strength starch then spread them in wide circles on the grass to dry stiff and scratchy.

On Monday mornings in the fall, I pulled on my red can-can, my white can-can, then my blue can-can. Over these I spread my favorite blue cotton skirt gathered on a band at the waist. It hung down to midway between my knees and my bobby socks. The hem formed a full circle about my legs. The circle was about four feet in diameter. The bigger the better.

I cinched my waist with a plastic belt three inches wide. The idea was to pull the belt as tight as possible and still breathe. (Tiny waists were the fad.) I buttoned all but the top buttons on my blue and white checked blouse. I rolled up once the elbow length sleeves and turned up my peter pan collar at the back of my neck. Around my neck, I knotted a blue silky neckerchief then pulled the knot to the side. I tied another blue neckerchief into a bow at the top of my long pony tail then combed my curly bangs.

"Bus is coming," Mom would yell from the foot of the stairs.

I grabbed my black letter sweater with the red school letter above the pocket. Picking up my small billfold bulging with pictures, lipstick, comb, mirror, notes, and sometimes money, I dashed downstairs.

Linda and I would give Mom a swift kiss good-bye then would dart for the yellow school bus waiting at the end of our graveled lane.

When winter came, we wore circular felt skirts over our stiff can-cans. My favorite skirt was aqua. A big white poodle was appliqued on the left side of my skirt and sat near the hem.

Twin sweater sets came on the scene. My short-sleeved pink pullover was worn under its matching long-sleeved cardigan sweater. For a new fad, girls sometimes wore the cardigans buttoned backwards. It was difficult to tell if we were coming or going.

Wool straight skirts with kick pleats in the back became the style. Dad protested. "No girl of mine needs to wear her skirts too tight."

"Oh, Dad," I groaned. "Your idea of a good fit is when I can shove both arms into either side of my skirt."

It was against school rules for girls to wear slacks during school hours.

After school, I wore pedal pushers. They stopped just below my knees. Mine were shiny cotton made for weekly ironing. My longer slacks were called torador pants. The pant leg hems fit snug about my ankles. If I sat down or bent over the pant legs rode up on the calves of my legs and caught there until I pulled them down to my bobby socks again. I spent more time pulling down my pant legs than I spent in an upright walking position.

Most teen-age boys wore khaki wash pants to school. The slacks came in tan, green, or blue and sported a belt buckle in the back for no reason at all. (Unless getting caught in chair backs was its purpose.)

A majority of the guys wore their short cropped hair held stiffly vertical with butch wax.

No boy was to come to school without a belt in his pants loops. They were not to walk the halls with their shirts unbuttoned. A T-shirt was not acceptable school attire.

Some guys strived to dress like "harley rats." Their hair was longer and greased back. They wore blue jeans, black engineer boots, and black leather jackets. They could be spotted a mile away. That was the whole idea.

But no long side burns. No long, long hair. No mustaches. No beards. If so, no school.

Summer time meant swimming time—but not before I was thirteen. It took years for me to overcome a fear of the water. In our backyard, Dad filled an oval horse tank with water for us to splash about in. Gradually, I smothered my fright. I held my breath, ducked under the water, and came up alive. Much to my surprise.

Linda and I played daily in the oversized tank. We learned to float on our stomachs then moved on to simple dog paddles. All feats were performed in our rusty horse tank.

Linda knew no fear of water-which sometimes led to precarious situations.

Linda was barely three feet tall when she yelled to Dad. "Here I come."

She jumped into the water at the end of a pier. The water was ten feet deep. Dad was swimming

fifty feet away. He fairly flew through the water to get TO Linda. She waited for him on the bottom. She couldn't swim. She couldn't float. she couldn't even struggle to the top of the water for air. But as she had expected, Dad was there to help her.

Together, Linda and I graduated from the backyard tank to cousin Kathlene and Jean's pond. Dad served as our instructor-playmate through the overhand stroke, side stroke, and the back stroke. He added his motorboat stroke (made by vigorously splashing with hands clenched above head) and the whale stroke (a back stroke with water spouting from the mouth). I didn't care much for Dad's inventive strokes.

Mother always sat on the grassy shore and watched us in the water. "Mom, why don't you come in? The water's fine." Her answer was always the same. "You **know** I get sea sick in the bath tub."

Mother and I struggled with differing points of view during my teen-age years. I wanted to go to all school and extra-ciricular activities. It was devastating to miss any school ball game at home or away.

Mother couldn't understand my involvement in a busy activity schedule: student council, Pep Club, band, stage band, Girls Athletic Association, Homecoming committees, prom committees, class play, National Honor Society, band head majorette.

Time and again after a heated discussion with me, she threw up her hands and said, "Why do you have to be in everything?"

"I have to go."

"Nancy, we live ten miles in the country. It's not a matter of life and death."

"To me, it is." Then came my tears.

Dad entered the argument. He spoke to Mother in low tones. Later, he turned to me and said, "Going is important to you?"

I nodded.

"Your Mom and I agree. You can go."

"Why does she have to be in everything," muttered Mother. "I wasn't in anything but orchestra when I was in high school."

Four years later when Linda became a high school cheerleader, Mother took it all in stride without protest. The first teenager in the house had broken her in to go, go, go.

What to do with a teenager in the house? Grin and bear it. Survive, survive, survive.

21
Dates, Watermelon Or Squash

The dates were double on a Saturday night in October. My date and I sat in the back seat of the car. My friend, Julie, rode close beside her date who was driving the car. We were on our way to my house after a weiner roast and hayride. My date, Dick, said "Isn't that a watermelon patch on the other side of that fence?"

"I don't know," said Joe. "It's hard to tell in the dark."

"Stop the car, Joe," said Dick. "I'll climb over the fence and get us a ripe watermelon to eat."

"I'll go with you," said Joe. He stopped the car on the country road. Both guys got out and disappeared over the fence into darkness.

Julie and I waited in the car with the motor running.

Soon, Dick and Joe jumped back over the fence. They scurried to the front of the car. Both of them carried a big round object in their arms. "We got watermelon," said Dick.

"Turn on the head lights, Julie. We'll cut out the hearts. Get ready for a bit of juicy red watermelon," shouted Joe.

Julie turned on the lights. Orange and yellow reflected light instead of red and green.

"Squash!" Yelled Dick. "These aren't watermelon, they're squash!"

I laughed and laughed at the look on their faces.

Between giggles, Julie said, "You can take me on a date any time, Joe. But no more watermelon or squash, please. It's too funny."

When the dating stage arrived at our household, Mother and Dad set down strict rules:

1-One date a week either on Friday night, Saturday night or Sunday afternoon.

2-No dates alone until the age of 16. (In actuality, I was 15 years 7 months.)

3-Wear dresses on dates unless plans call for slacks. No shorts!

4-Don't spend too much of a date's money.

5-Don't ride in a boy's car unless Mother and Dad know about it.

6-Don't park on country roads. If sitting in the car is necessary, do so in the driveway.

7-Don't stay out after midnight unless on extra special occasions with prior parental permission.

Once I broke dating rules. My date and I doubled with another couple. We went on a late night hayride. The tractor driver traveled more country roads than we had expected to. It was a l-o-n-g ride. I got home at 1:30 a.m. I was scared.

Next morning, I explained and apologized to Mom and Dad. Dad said, "Since this is the first time you've been late, we'll give you another chance. Don't let it happen again."

I was grateful. I didn't let it happen again.

If I sat in the car with my date over half an hour Mom turned on the flood light. It illuminated the driveway. I knew the signal and acted quickly, "I've got to go in. Don't bother to walk me to the door. Good night."

One Halloweeen night, Dick (the boyfriend who later became my husband) said, "Nancy's never soaped windows. Tonight we'll show her how it's done. Right, gang?"

"Right," chimed four chums (two boys, two girls) riding with us in Dick's old 1948 Chevy.

Off we went.

Dick turned up a side street in Sullivan. He drove at a snail's pace. "Here's a nice dark spot," said Dick.

"Car parked on the right," whispered Rodney.

"Okay, Rod. It's yours. Get the soap ready," said Dick. He turned out the headlights and eased his car up alongside the parked car. Rodney reached through the open window and soaped like crazy.

A front porch light came on in a blaze. A deep voice shouted, "What's going on out there?"

"Oh, no," said Rodney. "Let's get out of here. That's the deputy sheriff."

Dick's car shot down the street and around a corner. He turned on the headlights. "I'm taking you home," he said to me. "Could be trouble."

"Don't look now," I said. "Trouble's right behind us."

Sure enough. The deputy sheriff's car was closing in. The soaped window on his car hadn't slowed him down.

Dick pulled over to the side of the road. He rolled down his window and waited.

An angry deputy sheriff peered in and memorized six scared faces. "Who soaped my windows?"

No one said a word.

He turned to Dick. "Don't you know I could give you a ticket for driving without any headlights?"

"Yes sir."

"Where are you going now?"

"Home sir."

"See that you do." He stomped away.

One window soaping spree was enough to last me a life time.

Later, when I told Mom and Dad of our brush with the law, Mom frowned and Dad chuckled. I had learned long ago to always be the first to tell troublesome news. It was better to get it over with. Besides, Mother and Dad were more upset if they heard bad news about me from other people first.

High School Homecomings came in October. Pre-homecoming plans led to busy, busy days. In 1956, our class window won first place: We May be Green, but We've got the Queen. I worked hard on the committee. I was the one who made an imitation Algebra book and spelled it Algerba!

In 1957, our parade float carrying the queen candidate took first place: Sweet Old-fashioned Girl.

In 1958, our queen candidate was homecoming queen: Howdy Doody, Vote for Judy. (I was the chairman of the advertising committee. We campaigned with telephone calls, loud speakers on cars and posters for miles around.)

Homecoming 1959 was our final year. Our window on the square didn't win. Our float didn't win. Our queen didn't win. At least, the football players won the homecoming game.

The homecoming dance began after the football game. In my Junior year, I chose an aqua brocade dress to wear to the dance. It had a gored skirt, long sleeves and a scooped neckline trimmed in white fake fur. I glided into the decorated gym on the arm of my date delighted with my unusual dress.

Across the way stood a blonde. Her dress was identical to mine. Worse yet she looked better in her dress than I did in mine. From that moment on, I hid behind my date and stayed away from the blonde.

Dick became my steady boyfriend. His old Chevy was notorious for making strange noises, dying and running out of gas.

At first I thought Dick was up to one of his tricks when the car coughed, sputtered then died. One look at Dick's face told me it was no joke. We were having car trouble again. We'd walk to a telephone and call his dad or mine—whichever lived closer to the stalled car.

The big dance of the school year was Prom. I went twice; junior and senior years. Both times Dick was my escort.

As Juniors, Dick and I decorated for days. The gymnasium was transformed into 'An Evening in Paris' complete with flower carts, sidewalk cafes and the Eifal Tower standing ceiling high in the middle of the (basket ball) court. We were exhausted the night of the prom.

He wore a white dinner jacket. I wore a pink strapless ballerina length formal. Rows of chiffon ruffles circled the skirt.

Before the prom, I asked Mom, "May we go to the post prom celebration after the Prom?"

"Where is it?" asked Mother.

"At the Country Club."

"A post prom at the Country Club? You know what I think of a Country Club."

"All the kids are going," I said.

She talked it over with Dad. Finally, she said, "You may go to the Post Prom party, Nancy. But be home by two-o-clock."

"Ah Mom," I moaned. "No one else will leave that early."

"I said two-o-clock and I meant it."

"Yes, Mother."

After an eventful prom, I was thankful for strict parents as I ascended the stairs to my room at 2:00 a.m. I was too tired to stay any longer at the party. And I didn't have to admit it to my date or anyone. All I had to say was "You know Mom and Dad. They said two-o-clock. They set the rules. I follow them."

Let me explain part of the eventful prom night. Halfway through the dance, the musicans called a 15 minute intermission. Dick climbed into his dad's 1953 green Buick. I snuggled up close beside him. We went to the A&W stand for two frosty mugs of root beer on a warm May night.

We finished our drinks and had five minutes of intermission to spare. "Let's ride around the square a couple of times before we go back to the dance," said Dick.

"Okay," I agreed.

Once around we made it fine. On the second time around the square, a man in uniform yelled, "Hey, you in the green buick. Come down to police headquarters."

We recognized him as the night radio man for the police department. What was wrong?

Dick drove to headquarters. "I wonder if something happened at home," he said.

Inside the station, Mr. Withers said to Dick, "Where were you one hour ago?"

"At the prom, sir."

"Are you sure?"

"Yes, sir." Where else would we be in Sullivan dressed in formal attire?

At that moment, the police chief walked in. "What's going on here, Withers?"

"I caught those car thieves. That's the stolen

green buick outside."

"Withers, you'd better get back to your radio. We found the green buick abandoned on the south side of town.

Withers ducked his head and double-timed it out the door.

"Sorry, kids," said the chief. "Go on back to your prom and have a good time."

We did but fast. Not too fast though. One brush with the long arm of the law was enough for an evening.

The next year before Senior Prom, I asked, "How late this year, Mom and Dad?"

"You're seventeen now. Use your own judgement," said Dad.

Dick and I were elected king and queen of the Prom. I was crowned by the Junior class president. The current homecoming queen crowned Dick. They each claimed the coronation dance.

Dick swung and swayed to the music with a stiffness of the neck. He struggled to keep a tiny crown perched on top of his head. Meanwhile, there I was all smiles. Why? Because that's all anyone could see of my face. The too-big crown circled my eyes. You guessed it! Dick's crown was the Queen's; mine was the King's.

114

Before the next dance, we switched crowns. But not before the gymnasium of dancers dissolved with laughter at the sight we made. Dick and I laughed hardest of all. We knew the advantages of laughing at ourselves. If we hadn't laughed **with** others at ourselves, we would have been miserable embarassed while others laughed at our expense.

Senior Prom night, May sixth, Dick gave me a solitaire diamond ring for my left finger. We reigned at the dance then at Post Prom held in the Country Club. When did I get home? Two-o-clock in the morning.

Being free to choose my own curfew was a grand idea. I just happened to choose that time to go home. I was pooped! If staying at a party when you're pooped is someone's idea of freedom and fun, more power to them-they may need it-but count me out. Dick agreed with me.

Our Senior Class presented a play called **Desperate Ambrose**. I was cast as a comical character named Posie who was the heroine's black maid.

After one month of nightly practices, performance night arrived. Backstage, I peeked out at the capacity crowd packed into the gym. Mom, Dad and Linda sat front row center.

I turned around and gazed at my classmates. Beth, the heroine, was beautiful in her long flowing yellow dress. Her hair hung in ringlets riminiscent of the early 1800s style. Sarah, her play-sister, stood beside Beth in splendid blue. Sarah's dark brown hair was swept high off her neck into shimmering curls. Stage make-up emphasized their beauty.

From a mirror that hung on the west wall backstage, my reflection stared back at me. There I was. As usual, no beauty. But this time much worse. What would the audience think of me? My face, arms and hands shone black against my plain grey dress and white apron. A brush might never go through my hair again. I had poured a bottle of black rinse on my medium length locks then wound them on tiny metal rollers tight against my head. When I removed the rollers my hair remained kinky against my scalp.

Tears filled my eyes. What an ugly sight I made. That was me: never the pretty one; never the star; always the clown. If I had to be a funny maid, I might as well make the best of it.

The curtain rose. Act one began. Our play was a hit and a financial success. Later, to my surprise, many people congratulated me. "You were hilarious" "Funny! Funny!" "Your make-up was perfect for the part, Nancy."

My knowledge grew a little toward understanding and acceptance that night. People enjoyed laughing far better than they enjoyed looking.

Never again would I waste my time wishing for something I would never have. (Well—hardly ever wishing.) Instead, I'd spend my time developing the assets the good Lord saw fit to plant inside my brain instead of upon my body.

Aunt Mabel hired me as her assistant when I was 15. I worked in her beauty shop every other Saturday. During the summer my job grew to every Saturday as well as Fridays.

The summer I was 16, I worked four days a week for Aunt Mabel. After high school graduation, I enrolled as an apprentice beauty culturist for one year of study combined with work under the direction of Aunt Mabel.

At the end of my apprenticeship I passed state board at Springfield, Illinois. I became a cosmotoligist licensed by the state.

About my part-time job in high school, Mom said, "It costs more than Nancy earns to drive the car to and from work."

She was correct. But experience was priceless.

So was the beauty shop gossip.

Beauty shops are great gossip grab bags. Naive Nancy learned plenty in record time. I thought when people married they were loyal and faithful to each other 'till death do they part'.

I soon discovered that if everyone felt the same as I did there were people in town dying a dozen deaths. I made another discovery. Don't repeat what's heard in the Beauty Shop unless it's proven fact. If gossip was true, I battled against wanting to tell and trying not to.

May, 1960, arrived as any May may come with showers, sunshine and flowers. It brought me sadness. I was graduating. I didn't want to graduate. I loved high school. What lay ahead?

For one whole evening, I cried alone in my room. I graduated in grey and wept in the receiving line.

Reading books was my favorite pastime. Mother didn't mind my reading but she **did** object to my complete concentration.

"Nancy. Nancy. NANCY," she called. Then Mom sighed and said, "Nancy's got her nose in a book again. She'll never hear me. I'll do it myself."

Getting out of chores was the best reason I knew to build up the power of concentration.

I stuck with one boyfried in high school; Linda had

many. I didn't go to college; Linda went for one year. I rebelled and fought for independence when I was 14; Linda waited until she went away to college at 18. Away from home, she rebelled and fought for independence.

There wasn't much to do on dates in Sullivan. We bowled or went to the drive-in movies or stayed at my house and watched television with Mom, Dad and Linda.

Just before her death in 1954, Grandma Lane persuaded Dad to buy a television. "Maybe your girls will watch television, Dale," she said. "Then they won't get hurt riding calves or driving tractors."

Dad bought a black and white television in a blonde cabinet.

Grandma was happy. So were we. Watching Mickey Mouse Club was fun. Then there was Sky King, Roy Rogers and Dale Evans, Lassie, Lucy and Desi, Hit Parade, Ed Sullivan, The Whistler and Dragnet to name a few. We still had time to ride calves and drive tractors.

"Remember, Girls," said Dad to Linda and me before we went out on a date. "If you must sit in the car with your boyfriend, Do it in the driveway. Then, if you ever need dear old Dad, just yell. I'll come running."

Dates were fun so long as they stayed away from watermelon or squash.

22
Dearly Beloved

I graduated from high school third and fifth in a class of 90 students. How's that, you say? Two girls tied for Valedictorians; two girls were Salutatorians; next was me. That's third and fifth anyway you look at it.

Soon after graduation, my days were filled with wedding plans, preparations and showers. Dick and I set our wedding date for Sunday, August 7th at our mutual church in Sullivan.

"I want five people at the wedding," said Dick. "You, me, two witnesses and the preacher."

"What about your folks and mine?" I asked.

"Okay. Okay. Them, too."

"And your sister. I have to ask my aunts and uncles. What about yours?"

"Do you know what you're saying?" asked Dick. "My Dad has eight living brothers and sisters. Your Dad has seven. My Mom has five. Then there are friends, former classmates, the people I work with at the bank and on and on and on. We'll run out of room in the church."

We finally settled on approximately 100 guests. Dad helped us decide. He said, "Your mom and I'll give you five hundred dollars. You can spend it all on the wedding or have what's left over to buy furniture."

We spent $100.00 on gown, veil, flowers, gifts and reception. The rest of Mom and Dad's gift helped furnish our first home in Sullivan.

I played in a softball tournament one week before the wedding. Our team, the Sullivan Panthers, dressed in orange and black uniforms. Team members' ages varied from 13 to infinity. I played second base and relief pitcher. Linda played short shortstop. Twice a week, all summer, we met competition at home or traveled to ball diamonds in surrounding cities, towns and villages to compete against their rival women's softball teams.

It was my final game. I didn't plan to play softball after Dick and I were married. He came to watch my game. Game officials needed a third base umpire. Dick was asked. He consented to do it.

The game got underway. We were behind four to one. I made it to second base. The batter hit a grounder to first. I flew for third. The first base-woman threw the softball toward third. The softball hit me in the back of my head. I fell across third base. Stars swam before my eyes.

Did Dick rush to my side, scoop me into his arms and call my name? No.

What did he do? He stood his ground and calmly said, "Runner safe. Time out."

The day before Dick and I were to be married, I asked Dad, "Will you help me move my things to our house in town?"

Without a word, Dad got up, went outside and backed the truck up to our front door at home.

"There's the truck," he said. "You'll have to load up by yourself. I can't help move one of my girls out."

August 7th arrived; the hottest August 7th I've ever survived. Ten minutes before time to walk down the aisle, I was dressing in a room at the church. Jayne, my friend, darted in. "I just saw Dick leave in his car," she panted.

Now what? I finished final preparations all the while wondering why the groom had left.

Jerry, our soloist, finished singing 'God Gave Me You!. Next, he sang 'I Love You Truly'. I waited with Dad, my sister (the maid of honor), and Dick's two nephews ages five and six. They were our double ring-bearers.

The sanctuary doors swung open on the organ's first note of 'Here Comes the Bride'.

There was Dick waiting for me at the altar. He'd made it back to his wedding after all.

Dad had said he hated to see me leave home but he all but ran down the aisle to give me away.

Much later, I asked Dick, "Where did you go ten minutes before the ceremony?"

"I had to go home," he said. "I forgot the marriage license."

Dick had been saving money for a honeymoon to the Wisconsin Dells 300 miles north. Two days before the wedding, he had his car checked. There was a crack in the crank case. It had to be fixed. The repair bill was high.

Our honeymoon was to Starved Rock State Park 80 miles away. We stayed two days.

One week in our new home rushed by. Rings built up around the bath tub. I hadn't noticed that when I took baths at home.

I scrubbed the tub. Mom stopped by an hour later. "A funny thing, Mom," I said. "Nobody cleaned my bath ring for me. I had to do it myself."

Mom cried. I had intended to make her laugh.

Four years later, in May, Linda graduated from Sullivan High School. She received the Outstanding Mathematics Award.

In the fall, she enrolled at the University of Illinois.

After one year, she returned home for the summer. A former classmate asked her for a date in June. In July, she stopped by as I was frying fish

for supper.

"Nancy, Calvin asked me to marry him. I said yes. I wanted you to be the first to know."

What a shock! I immediately dropped the skillet of frying grease. As I bent for it, grease flew in my face. I had to wear sunglasses for two weeks to protect my scorched eyes.

Two months later, on October 2nd, Linda and Calvin were married in our family church.

"Wilma and I'll give you five hundred dollars," said Dad to them. "Spend it however you want to."

Linda and Cal had a lovely wedding and reception with 100 guests and all the trimmings for $150.00. Dad gave her away. I was her matron of honor.

For both weddings, Mom said, "It's your wedding. You make all the plans. Just tell me what to do."

And that's what Linda and I did.

'Dearly Beloved' brought early marriages to two girls raised on a farm. Neither of us married farmers. Dick was in banking. Cal became a certified public accountant.

Whether at city or farm, it's in your power to be contented or dissatisfied; joyful or sorrowful; amused or abused.

Life will be filled with ups and downs. Don't ask 'Is that all there is?', make more of the moment, the hour, the day. Today won't pass this way again.

23
Time Flies

Time flies when you're having fun. In March of 1975, Mom and Dad celebrated their thirty-fifth wedding anniversary.

Dad still farms, but not as much as before (eighty acres this year). He still sees to thirty head of cattle, all descendants of Old Jerse.

Mom and Dad's garden is bigger than ever. The grandchildren and Grandpa have an arrangement to sell sweet corn every summer. Grandpa gathers the ripe sweet corn, sells it to the grandchildren for a penny an ear, and the kids in turn sell it to customers for seventy-five cents a baker's dozen.

Speaking of grandkids, there are five. Dick (my high school boyfriend) and I have been married fifteen years. Our daughter Jill is thirteen; sons Doug and Brad are eleven and eight respectively. Linda and Cal will soon be married ten years. Their daughter Kim is eight and son Jeff is seven.

Linda and her family recently moved from Terre Haute, Indiana to California. Mom and Dad are planning to make their first flight west to visit them as soon as all the cows have their calves. Dick, our three children, and I still reside in Sullivan.

Dad is still a joker. Anytime, anywhere, the grandkids expect anything. At Mom and Dad's house, there's a two-seater go-cart for the grandchildren. Dad made each of them a sled. But he didn't demonstrate how to use it in the snow as he did twenty years ago. He tells the same stories to the grandchildren as he told to his daughters. Mostly, he gets the same response, "Tell us another, Grandpa!"

The other day, Jill was heard to say, "Grandpa, are you **sure** that's a true story?"

Dad also made five pairs of stilts and five stick whistles.

Life goes on as the years zoom by. Life's a pleasure. Let us be entertained by its pleasantries, joys, and delights, large or small. Take time to remember. Sit back. Relax. Recall people, places, and things. Feel again emotions felt before. Live anew old memories.

Looking back with love, I see sacrifices my parents made for me. They didn't expect any thanks. I thank them just the same.

Looking back with understanding, I see rules and reprimands for my own good, although it didn't seem so then.

Looking back with responsibility, I see values measured in faith and hope not in dollars and cents and in hard work well done.

Live with love. And learn by looking back with laughter.